The Empire's Warning: What Rome's Fall Tells Us About the West Today

John Shenton

Published by John Shenton, 2024.

THE EMPIRE'S WARNING: WHAT ROME'S FALL TELLS US ABOUT THE WEST TODAY

First edition. October 5, 2024.

Copyright © 2024 John Shenton.

ISBN: 979-8227663481

Written by John Shenton.

Also by John Shenton

Business Plan Basics
The Bahamas - More Islands and Recipes Than You Expect!
Collected Musings from Bricks and Mortar to E-commerce
The Smart City Odyssey: Unveiling the Secrets to Traveller-Centric Software
The Dragon's Gambit: China's Bid for Global Dominance and the Western Response
Silent Weapon
Business Basics: Money Sources
Influx
Fried Chips
Mandates, Motors, and Misinformation
Echos of Orwell
Control and Chaos
The Empire's Warning: What Rome's Fall Tells Us About the West Today

Table of Contents

Introduction

Growing up in England, I was fortunate to have history practically on my doorstep. In my younger years, I walked along Hadrian's Wall many times, gazing out over the rugged landscape and imagining what it must have been like for Roman soldiers stationed there nearly two thousand years ago. The Roman presence in Britain always captivated me, particularly in places like *Vindolanda,* where the remnants of a once-great empire lie quietly beneath the soil, bearing witness to a time when the light of civilisation shone brightly in what was then a distant frontier of the Roman world.

My fascination with Rome deepened as I grew older, reading Edward Gibbon's monumental work, *The History of the Decline and Fall of the Roman Empire*, which remains, to my mind, one of the most significant historical analyses ever written. Gibbon's eloquence and keen insight into the slow erosion of Roman power, morality, and unity left an indelible mark on me. Since then, I have read countless other works on Rome both scholarly and fictional each offering a different facet of this once-mighty empire and the lessons it holds for our own time. It was a period of such richness and grandeur that, when it ended, the lights of civilisation dimmed across Europe for centuries.

In writing *The Empire's Warning: What Rome's Fall Tells Us About the West Today*, I have sought to draw direct comparisons between the collapse of the Roman Empire and the potential future of the West. We are at a critical juncture, and this book seeks to examine whether we are doomed to repeat history or if, unlike Rome, we can avoid a similar fate. I aim to explore this question through the lens of history but with an eye on the current geopolitical, social, and economic trends shaping the modern world.

The final chapter, *The Future of Western Civilisation: Decline or Transformation?* Is perhaps the most poignant of all. As I walked through those Roman ruins and read about the slow degradation of one of the greatest empires the world has ever known, I couldn't help but reflect on what lies ahead for our civilisation. The West like Rome in its prime once stood unchallenged in its power and influence. But today, we face a crossroads. Can we transform ourselves, adapting to the challenges of an increasingly complex world, or are we destined to follow Rome into history?

Drawing on historical patterns, I pose the question of whether decline is inevitable or if there exists the possibility for transformation. We stand on the precipice of immense geopolitical shifts, technological revolutions, and even the potential for a cultural renaissance. As with the Roman Empire in its final days, the future of Western civilisation may hinge on whether we can reimagine ourselves, rebalance our economies, reinvigorate our democracies, and rekindle the cultural vibrancy that once defined us.

This chapter also reflects on what a renewed Western society might look like a vision of resilient communities, stable economies, and thriving democracies. Or might we continue a path of moral, cultural, and economic decay as Gibbon suggested about Rome?

Before we reach that conclusion, however, the preceding chapters offer a deep dive into the root causes of both Rome's fall and the current Western predicament. In the chapter *Can Decline Be Reversed?* I explore the reforms of Diocletian and Constantine's efforts to save the Roman Empire that, while remarkable, ultimately failed. Can the West avoid the same outcome through a return to domestic manufacturing, educational reform, and technological innovation? These are the questions I pose, with the hope that we may find a way to arrest our potential decline.

I have also examined the collapse of public faith, which, as it did in Rome, plays a critical role in today's societal fragmentation. The loss of civic duty, religious fragmentation, and a disillusioned populace were harbingers of Rome's collapse, as I discuss in *The Collapse of Public Faith: Religion, Civic Duty, and Decline.* The parallels with the West today, where secularisation and distrust in institutions are rampant, cannot be ignored.

We can no longer afford to be complacent, and we certainly cannot ignore the lessons of history. Corruption, political instability, mass immigration, and military overstretch were the hallmarks of a declining Roman Empire, and in chapters such as *Economic and Political Corruption* and *Immigration and Integration*, I detail the dangerous similarities we face today. The very fabric of our societies' moral, political, and military appears to be fraying at the edges, much like it did in late antiquity.

Ultimately, *The Empire's Warning* is not a tale of doom but of cautious optimism. It is a call to action, an invitation to learn from history rather than repeat it. Rome, for all its might, could not arrest its fall. But perhaps we, with the benefit of hindsight and foresight, can still steer our civilisation away from the brink and into a future of transformation rather than decline.

Whether the West chooses a path of reinvention or resignation will be the defining question of our age.

John Shenton

Chapter 1: The Empire at its Zenith: A Comparison of Rome and the Modern West

At its height, the Roman Empire was an unrivalled superpower, a colossus that spanned from the British Isles to the fringes of the Middle East, shaping the world in ways that continue to resonate today. It was a civilisation that excelled in military might, cultural sophistication, governance, and economic dominance. When we examine the West today, particularly the United States, United Kingdom, Canada, and Western Europe we see a striking parallel. In the years following the Second World War, these nations stood at the pinnacle of global influence, embodying many of the same qualities that defined the Roman Empire during its zenith. But, as history warns, empires do not last forever.

This chapter draws a comparison between Rome at its peak and the modern West, exploring the various achievements that defined these societies. By looking back at Rome's golden age, we can better understand the current position of the West and appreciate the factors that made it dominant, but also begin to detect the seeds of decline.

Rome at its Peak: A Beacon of Civilisation

The Roman Empire reached its zenith during the reign of the "Five Good Emperors" (96–180 AD), a period characterised by political stability, economic prosperity, military success, and unmatched cultural flourishing. Rome was not just a vast territorial entity; it was a civilisation that shaped the very foundation of Western culture.

At the heart of Roman greatness was its military. With legions stationed across three continents, Rome possessed an army that was highly disciplined, professionally trained, and unmatched in its time. The Empire's military might allowed it to secure vast territories, defend against external threats, and maintain internal stability. But Rome's dominance was not solely the product of brute force; it was a product of an extraordinary system of governance and the projection of Roman values.

Roman law, governance, and infrastructure were critical to maintaining this far-flung empire. Roads spanned the Empire, connecting provinces and facilitating trade, communication, and military deployment. Aqueducts brought water into cities, while monumental architecture symbolised Roman power and glory. The administrative prowess of the Roman state was also remarkable. Local governors ensured the smooth functioning of distant provinces, while a relatively standardised legal system provided order and stability.

Culturally, Rome absorbed and repurposed the best elements of the societies it conquered, from Greek philosophy to Egyptian science. It became a melting pot of ideas, art, and learning, establishing a cultural hegemony that persisted long after its political power waned. The Pax Romana, or "Roman Peace," allowed for unparalleled trade and economic growth, not just within the Empire but with distant lands like China and India. Rome's economy, bolstered by agricultural productivity and trade, flourished, and its currency, the denarius, was widely recognised and trusted.

The Modern West at its Zenith: Post-War Dominance

The decades following the Second World War saw the rise of a new set of global powers the United States, the United Kingdom, Canada, and Western Europe. The post-war West, much like Rome at its zenith, enjoyed a period of unparalleled dominance. Economically, militarily, and culturally, the Western world established itself as the de facto leader of global affairs. There are clear parallels to Rome in this period of supremacy, but it also raises important questions about the sustainability of this dominance.

Economically, the West, and particularly the United States, became the global economic engine. The Bretton Woods system, established in 1944, anchored the global economy to the US dollar, much like the Roman denarius had been a trusted currency across the ancient world. The post-war economic boom, especially in the US and Western Europe, saw unprecedented levels of productivity, industrial output, and technological innovation. The Marshall Plan helped rebuild Europe, leading to strong economic alliances and the birth of institutions such as NATO and the European Economic Community, which would later evolve into the European Union.

Technologically, the West led the world. From the space race, culminating in the US moon landing in 1969, to the rapid advances in computing and telecommunications, the Western world became synonymous with innovation and progress. Much like Rome had harnessed the best engineering and scientific minds of its time to build aqueducts, roads, and cities, the modern West developed the infrastructure of a globalised world airports, highways, and digital networks that facilitated not only commerce but also the spread of Western culture.

Culturally, the West became the dominant force on the global stage. Hollywood movies, British literature, American music, and Western fashion shaped global tastes and values. The spread of liberal democratic ideals free markets, human rights, and the rule of law became the hallmark of the Western-led world order, much like the spread of Roman law and governance had shaped the ancient world.

Militarily, the West established a dominance that mirrored Rome's legions. The United States, with its vast nuclear arsenal and technologically superior military, emerged as the world's policeman, a role Britain had once played in the 19th century. NATO, a transatlantic military alliance, ensured Western military superiority over the Eastern bloc during the Cold War, while the projection of military power in conflicts from Korea to the Gulf War solidified the West's global hegemony.

Parallels in Economic Dominance

Just as Rome was the economic hub of the ancient world, the post-war West established itself as the centre of global commerce. Rome's economy was underpinned by a vast network of trade routes, connecting the provinces and with distant lands. Goods from as far away as India, Arabia, and sub-Saharan Africa found their way to Roman markets. This vast trading network brought wealth and luxury to the Empire's urban elite, fuelling a consumer-driven economy much like that of the modern West.

In a similar vein, the modern West, particularly through institutions like the World Bank and the International Monetary Fund, established a global economic order that benefited from globalisation. Trade agreements such as NAFTA and the European Single Market allowed for the free flow of goods, capital, and labour across borders. Western corporations became multinational behemoths, controlling vast supply chains that spanned the globe.

Both Rome and the modern West built their economic systems on exploitation to some degree. For Rome, it was slavery and the extraction of resources from conquered territories. For the modern West, it has been the exploitation of cheap labour in developing countries and the extraction of natural resources. This economic model, while highly successful in the short term, raises important questions about sustainability questions that both Rome and the West eventually had to confront.

Military Supremacy: The Legions and the Western Alliance

Rome's military might was the foundation of its empire. The legions were not just soldiers; they were engineers, builders, and symbols of Roman authority. They secured the borders, quelled internal revolts, and projected Roman power across the known world. The Pax Romana, a period of relative peace and stability, was maintained through the constant presence of Roman military power. The legions were the sword and shield of the Roman state, and without them, the empire would have collapsed much sooner than it did.

In the modern West, military supremacy has similarly underpinned global dominance. The United States, with its vast network of overseas military bases and unmatched naval power, has played a role similar to that of Rome. NATO, with its collective security agreement, has acted as a deterrent against external threats, much like the Roman military alliances and client states did in antiquity. Western military intervention in conflicts from the Balkans to the Middle East has been a demonstration of this power.

Yet, just as Rome's military dominance was not infinite, cracks have begun to appear in the modern Western alliance. The protracted wars in Iraq and Afghanistan have revealed the limitations of military power in achieving political goals. Rome too, at the height of its power, struggled to maintain control over distant provinces like Judea and Britannia, where local resistance proved difficult to crush. As we look to the future, the question arises: Can the modern West maintain its military supremacy indefinitely, or will it, like Rome, become overstretched and vulnerable?

Cultural Influence: Rome's Legacy and the West's Soft Power

Rome's cultural influence far outlasted its political dominance. Latin, the language of the Romans, became the lingua franca of the Western world for centuries after the Empire's fall. Roman law became the foundation of legal systems across Europe, and Roman architecture and art were emulated by subsequent civilisations. Even today, in the fields of literature, philosophy, and governance, Roman ideas continue to exert a profound influence.

Similarly, the modern West has wielded an unparalleled degree of soft power. Hollywood films, American music, British literature, and European art have shaped global tastes and values in ways that are difficult to overstate. The West's cultural hegemony, like Rome's, has been based on more than just military or economic power it has been a force of persuasion, a projection of ideals and values that others aspire to.

However, just as Rome's cultural influence began to fade as its political power waned, there were signs that the West's soft power was also diminishing. The rise of alternative centres of cultural influence, such as China and India, suggests that the Western cultural dominance that defined the 20th century may not last indefinitely. As new powers emerge, the West may find itself increasingly challenged in the realm of ideas, values, and cultural leadership.

The Seeds of Decline

While the comparison between Rome at its zenith and the modern West reveals many similarities, it is important to recognise that the seeds of decline were already present within both. For Rome, internal divisions, economic instability, and the overextension of its military eventually led to its downfall. Corruption, a widening gap between the rich and poor, and a failure to address systemic issues hastened its collapse.

As we continue our exploration of the parallels between the fall of Rome and the potential decline of the modern West, it is essential to acknowledge a profound shift that has already begun to take shape: the rise of alternative centres of cultural influence, particularly in the East. During the height of the Roman Empire, its cultural dominance was virtually unchallenged in the Western world. However, as the Empire began to weaken, other regions, particularly those in the East, started to assert their own cultural identities and began to challenge Rome's supremacy. Today, the rise of China and India offers a similar parallel. These nations are increasingly asserting their cultural values and leadership on the world stage, suggesting that the Western cultural dominance that defined much of the 20th century may not endure indefinitely.

The Shift in Cultural Hegemony

Cultural influence, or "soft power," is not static. It ebbs and flows with the rise and fall of nations and civilisations. Just as Rome's cultural legacy was later challenged by the emergence of Byzantine, Persian, and Islamic influences, the cultural dominance of the modern West specifically the United States, the United Kingdom, and Western Europe is facing increasing competition from non-Western powers. The 20th century was an era of Western cultural hegemony. The English language became the global lingua franca, Hollywood defined global entertainment, and Western ideals of democracy, individualism, and free-market capitalism were exported and adopted in many parts of the world.

But in the 21st century, the global cultural landscape is shifting. The economic rise of China and India has been mirrored by their growing cultural influence. As these nations assert themselves economically, they are also increasingly pushing back against the Western cultural norms that once held unrivalled sway. For the first time in decades, the West is facing a significant challenge to its soft power dominance, and this may have profound implications for global cultural leadership in the coming years.

China's Cultural Reassertion: The Middle Kingdom Ascends

China's cultural reassertion can be understood in the context of its economic and geopolitical resurgence. The Chinese Communist Party (CCP) has long recognised the importance of soft power as a complement to its growing economic and military power. Beijing's ambitious global infrastructure project, the Belt and Road Initiative (BRI) has been framed not just as an economic venture but as a vehicle for exporting Chinese culture, values, and influence. Confucius Institutes have been established around the world to promote the study of Chinese language and culture, with the clear intention of shaping global perceptions of China.

This cultural outreach is an integral part of China's larger strategy to challenge Western ideological dominance. Chinese cinema, for example, is no longer confined to domestic audiences. Films such as *Wolf Warrior 2* a patriotic blockbuster represent a new narrative, one that promotes Chinese nationalism and casts China as a benevolent global power. Meanwhile, China's state media has expanded its reach through international channels like CGTN, which broadcasts news and cultural programming that counters Western narratives and promotes a distinctly Chinese perspective on global affairs.

One of the most striking aspects of China's cultural reassertion is its challenge to the notion that Western-style democracy and human rights are universal ideals. Chinese leaders have consistently argued that Western liberal democracy is not suited to China's unique historical and cultural context. Instead, they promote the "China model" a blend of authoritarian governance and state-directed capitalism as an alternative path to modernisation. This is a direct challenge to the Western idea that liberal democracy is the only legitimate form of governance, and it resonates in many parts of the developing world, where the failures of Western interventions are often viewed with scepticism.

China's growing influence in the realm of technology also plays a crucial role in shaping cultural norms. The rise of Chinese tech giants like Tencent, Alibaba, and ByteDance (owner of TikTok) has allowed China to export its technological innovations globally. Social media platforms and apps developed in China are shaping how young people around the world communicate, consume content, and interact with one another. This is a sharp departure from the late 20th century when Silicon Valley dominated the digital landscape. With China's advancements in artificial intelligence, 5G, and digital surveillance, the country is exporting not only its technology but also its model of digital authoritarianism, which some governments may find appealing as an alternative to Western internet governance models that prioritise freedom of speech and privacy.

India's Cultural Renaissance: The World's Largest Democracy Rising

India, too, is experiencing a cultural renaissance, although its trajectory differs markedly from China's. As the world's largest democracy and a nation with a rich and ancient cultural heritage, India is asserting itself on the global stage, not through authoritarianism, but by leveraging its democratic institutions and vibrant, pluralistic society. The rise of India is as much about reclaiming its cultural heritage as it is about asserting its economic and political power.

Bollywood, India's film industry, has long been a cultural force across Asia, Africa, and the Middle East, but in recent years, it has garnered increasing attention in the West. The global popularity of Indian music, dance, and fashion has expanded beyond the Indian diaspora, reaching mainstream audiences in Europe and the Americas. Meanwhile, Indian cuisine has become a global culinary staple, and yoga, a centuries-old Indian practice, has been adopted by millions worldwide. These cultural exports are not mere entertainment or trends; they are carriers of Indian values and philosophies, subtly challenging Western conceptions of health, beauty, and spirituality.

India's political and cultural reassertion is also being championed by its current leadership. Under Prime Minister Narendra Modi, India has embraced a more assertive form of nationalism that seeks to project Indian culture and values on the world stage. Modi's emphasis on "Make in India" and "Digital India" reflects a desire to position the country as a hub of innovation and technology, much like China. India is increasingly seen as a global player in the tech industry, particularly in software development and information technology. Its large and youthful population is expected to play a key role in shaping the future of digital culture.

India's position as the world's largest democracy gives it a unique form of soft power that distinguishes it from China. While China promotes an authoritarian model, India's democratic system, flawed as it may be, offers a counter-narrative. India can appeal to nations that are wary of both Western paternalism and Chinese authoritarianism by offering an alternative that embraces both modernisation and democracy. This allows India to exert cultural influence not only in the developing world but also in the West, where concerns about authoritarianism and the erosion of democratic values are growing.

The Challenge to Western Ideals: A Multipolar Cultural World

The rise of China and India marks the emergence of a multipolar cultural world, one in which Western ideals and values are no longer universally accepted or unchallenged. For much of the 20th century, Western liberalism was seen as the inevitable endpoint of human development, particularly after the collapse of the Soviet Union. The "end of history," as it was famously described by political scientist Francis Fukuyama, seemed to suggest that liberal democracy, free markets, and individual rights were the pinnacle of human civilisation.

However, the 21st century has shown that history is far from over. As China promotes its model of authoritarian modernisation and India reasserts its cultural heritage, the world is witnessing the rise of alternative ideologies and values. In many parts of the developing world, there is a growing sense that Western liberalism is not the only path to progress. The failures of Western interventions in Iraq, Afghanistan, and Libya, as well as the financial crises that have rocked Europe and the United States, have eroded the appeal of the Western model. In its place, nations are looking to China and India as models for economic development and cultural identity.

This shift poses a significant challenge to the West. For decades, Western nations have promoted a set of values of democracy, human rights, and free markets as universal. But the rise of China and India suggests that the world is moving towards a more pluralistic understanding of culture, governance, and progress. As these nations continue to assert their influence, the West may find itself increasingly challenged in the realm of ideas and values. The notion of a single, dominant cultural model once held by Rome and, more recently, by the West may give way to a more fragmented global cultural landscape.

Cultural Leadership in the Digital Age

The rise of alternative centres of cultural influence also highlights the role of technology in shaping cultural power. In the digital age, cultural influence is not confined by geography. The internet has created a global platform where ideas, art, and values can be disseminated instantaneously. This has allowed nations like China and India to project their cultural power far beyond their borders, challenging the West's traditional dominance in media, entertainment, and intellectual discourse.

Social media platforms, video-sharing sites, and digital streaming services have become the new battlegrounds for cultural leadership. China's TikTok has become one of the most popular social media platforms globally, allowing Chinese creators to influence global trends in music, fashion, and entertainment. Indian content creators, too, have found a global audience on platforms like YouTube, where they share everything from Bollywood dance tutorials to philosophical discourses on Hinduism and Indian spirituality.

As these digital platforms grow, the West's ability to control the global cultural narrative diminishes. In previous centuries, cultural influence was often tied to physical artefacts books, films, and music albums that were produced and distributed by Western companies. But in the digital age, anyone with an internet connection can become a cultural creator, and new narratives can emerge from the most unexpected places. The decentralisation of cultural production means that the West must now compete with a global chorus of voices, many of which are questioning the dominance of Western ideals.

The Future of Cultural Power

The rise of alternative centres of cultural influence particularly China and India suggests that the global cultural landscape is shifting in ways that could significantly diminish the West's soft power dominance. While the West will likely remain a major cultural force for the foreseeable future, it is increasingly clear that it no longer holds a monopoly on cultural leadership. Just as Rome's cultural legacy was challenged by the rise of new powers in the East, so too is the modern West facing a challenge from the re-emergence of ancient civilisations with their rich cultural traditions.

This multipolar cultural world presents both challenges and opportunities. The West can no longer assume that its values and ideals will be universally embraced. Instead, it must engage with and adapt to a world where multiple cultural models coexist, each with its claims to legitimacy. Whether the West can successfully navigate this new cultural landscape will depend on its willingness to learn from other civilisations, embrace diversity, and remain open to new ideas.

The Future of Cultural Power and the West's Imperative to Preserve Its Heritage

While the rise of alternative centres of cultural influence, particularly in China and India, is undeniable, I firmly believe that the West cannot simply accept a future where its cultural and ideological dominance fades into the background. Unlike ancient Rome, which was eventually overwhelmed by external influences and internal disintegration, the modern West has the opportunity and indeed, the responsibility to resist a similar fate. The decline of Rome offers us a crucial lesson: a civilisation that fails to protect its core values and traditions is vulnerable to cultural erosion and eventual collapse.

The Western world's rise to global prominence was not an accident of history, nor merely the result of military conquest or economic power. It was underpinned by a unique cultural and philosophical framework, rooted in the Judeo-Christian tradition. This heritage shaped the moral, ethical, and legal foundations of Western societies, fostering a commitment to individual rights, the rule of law, and democratic governance. The Western conception of human dignity, personal liberty, and the inherent worth of every individual owes much to the Judeo-Christian worldview, which provided the moral scaffolding for the Enlightenment and the subsequent developments in political theory and human rights.

Rome, too, was once a bastion of cultural confidence, dominating the known world with its military might, governance, and sophisticated legal and architectural systems. Yet, as Rome expanded and absorbed new cultures, it gradually lost sight of its founding ideals. The influx of foreign customs, religions, and ideologies weakened the Roman identity, creating fractures within its social fabric. By the time of the late Empire, the Roman cultural legacy had been diluted to such an extent that it could no longer unify its citizens under a shared sense of purpose. The Western world today stands at a similar crossroads. The rise of alternative powers like China and India, each with their distinct cultural paradigms, poses a challenge not only to the West's influence but also to its identity.

The West, particularly in the post-World War II era, has been the epicentre of technological innovation, economic growth, and global cultural leadership. However, the erosion of its cultural self-confidence manifested in the rise of moral relativism, identity politics, and the rejection of its heritage threatens the very foundation that allowed it to flourish in the first place. If the West is to resist the fate of Rome, it must recognise the value of preserving its Judeo-Christian roots, which provided the ethical and moral compass that guided its ascent. The challenge is not to resist the influence of other cultures entirely but to balance this with a steadfast commitment to protecting its core values.

The Dangers of Cultural Relativism

One of the most significant threats to the West's cultural identity is the rise of cultural relativism the idea that no culture is inherently better or more valuable than any other. While this notion may appear tolerant or open-minded, it ultimately undermines the unique achievements of Western civilisation. Western society, built on the principles of individual rights, democracy, and free markets, has provided unprecedented levels of prosperity, freedom, and innovation. To abandon the philosophical underpinnings that made this possible is to risk the very future of Western civilisation.

Rome, in its later stages, suffered from a similar form of relativism. As it absorbed more and more foreign customs and religions, the once-cohesive Roman identity became fragmented. The old Roman virtues of *gravitas*, *virtus*, and *pietas* which emphasised duty, courage, and reverence were gradually replaced by a hodgepodge of conflicting beliefs. Christianity, once a persecuted minority religion, became the state religion under Emperor Constantine, marking a decisive shift in Roman identity. While the adoption of Christianity may have saved Rome spiritually, it also signalled the end of traditional Roman civic values. By the time of the Empire's collapse, Rome had lost the cultural coherence necessary to unite its people in the face of external and internal challenges.

In the modern West, the rise of competing value systems whether from secular humanism, radical political ideologies, or foreign cultural influences threatens to do the same. Western nations increasingly find themselves divided over fundamental issues of identity, morality, and the role of the state. The embrace of multiculturalism, while offering many benefits, has also led to a dilution of Western values. In some cases, this has resulted in a reluctance to defend the cultural heritage that made the West successful. There is a growing tendency, particularly among Western intellectual elites, to view Western civilisation not as something to be proud of but as something to be apologised for. This trend, if left unchecked, could mirror Rome's gradual loss of cultural self-confidence.

Preserving the Judeo-Christian Tradition

The preservation of Western culture, therefore, requires a reassertion of its Judeo-Christian heritage. This is not to suggest that other cultures or religions should be excluded or marginalised. On the contrary, Western societies have long thrived on their openness to new ideas and the contributions of diverse peoples. However, this openness must be balanced by a commitment to protecting the core values that define the West. Without this, the West risks becoming a cultural blank slate upon which any ideology whether authoritarian or anarchic can be imposed.

The Judeo-Christian tradition has provided a moral framework that emphasises the dignity of the individual, the importance of justice, and the need for compassion and charity. These principles have shaped the West's legal systems, its political institutions, and its social norms. The Enlightenment, often seen as a secular break from religious tradition, was deeply influenced by Judeo-Christian ideas. Thinkers such as John Locke, Montesquieu, and Adam Smith were all products of a cultural milieu steeped in Christian ethics, and their works laid the groundwork for modern democracy and capitalism.

If the West abandons its Judeo-Christian heritage, it risks losing the moral clarity that has guided it through centuries of upheaval and change. Just as Rome, in its later years, lost the guiding principles that had made it great, the West today faces the danger of moral and cultural drift. In a world increasingly dominated by competing ideologies from Chinese authoritarianism to radical Islamism to the secular materialism of global capitalism the West must offer a compelling alternative. That alternative lies in its heritage, in the values of freedom, justice, and individual dignity that have been passed down through the centuries.

Resisting Cultural Overwhelm

The Western world should not only recognise the rise of alternative cultural powers but also actively resist being overwhelmed by them. This is not a call for isolationism or xenophobia, but rather for a healthy cultural self-confidence. The West has much to offer the world, but it can only do so if it retains a clear sense of its own identity. The Roman Empire, in its later years, became so focused on incorporating foreign customs and managing its far-flung territories that it lost sight of what had made it great in the first place. In much the same way, the modern West risks being consumed by a desire to accommodate every external influence, to the detriment of its cultural integrity.

China and India, despite their economic and cultural ascendance, remain deeply committed to their traditions. China's government actively promotes Confucian values and Communist Party ideology, while India draws on its ancient Hindu heritage to shape its national identity. These nations have not abandoned their cultural roots in the face of modernity; instead, they have adapted and reasserted them in the global arena. The West should take note. Rather than allowing itself to be overwhelmed by the rising tide of foreign ideologies, the West must find ways to reassert its cultural heritage in a manner that is both confident and inclusive.

One way to achieve this is through education. The Western educational system has, in many ways, neglected to teach the younger generations about the values and principles that shaped Western civilisation. A renewed emphasis on the study of history, philosophy, and the great works of Western literature could help cultivate a sense of pride in the Western tradition. By understanding the intellectual and cultural foundations of the West, future generations can better appreciate the importance of preserving these values in the face of external challenges.

A Call to Action: Defend the Western Legacy

The decline of Rome offers a stark warning to the modern West: cultural complacency leads to decline. The rise of alternative powers like China and India should serve as a wake-up call. The West must not only recognise these emerging centres of influence but also resist being overwhelmed by them. The key to doing so lies in a renewed commitment to the Judeo-Christian heritage that gave rise to Western civilisation's most enduring achievements.

This is not a call for a return to the past, but rather a call to preserve the essential values that have guided the West through centuries of progress. The West must continue to innovate, to embrace new ideas, and to engage with the world. But it must do so from a position of strength, rooted in the knowledge of what made it great. Just as Rome might have avoided its fate had it retained a clear sense of its own identity, the West today can resist decline by reaffirming the cultural and moral foundations that led to its rise.

In the face of rising alternative powers, the West must defend its legacy, not by retreating into isolation, but by confidently asserting the values of freedom, democracy, and human dignity. These values, grounded in the Judeo-Christian tradition, remain as relevant today as they were centuries ago. If the West can do this, it will not only survive but thrive in a world of shifting power dynamics. The lessons of Rome are clear: cultural resilience is key to enduring greatness. The West, if it is to avoid Rome's fate, must reclaim its cultural heritage and protect the values that have sustained it through the ages.

Chapter 2: Signs of Decay: The Roman Empire and Present-Day Western Decline

In examining the rise and eventual decline of the Roman Empire, I am struck by how familiar many of the Empire's early warning signs of decay feel in the context of our modern-day Western societies. Just as Rome, at the height of its power, began to show cracks in its foundation, today we can observe several troubling parallels across the USA, UK, Canada, and Western Europe. In this chapter, I will explore these similarities, drawing on the Roman experience to better understand the present challenges we face and the potential trajectories our societies might follow if left unaddressed.

Political Corruption and Weakening Institutions

One of the earliest indicators of Rome's decline was the gradual erosion of its political institutions. Corruption became endemic, with public officials routinely placing personal gain above the needs of the Empire. The once-disciplined Senate, which had guided Rome through centuries of expansion and stability, increasingly became a battleground for factions vying for power. The very concept of public service was warped as positions within the government were bought and sold, and loyalty to the state gave way to loyalty to individual leaders or factions.

Similarly, today we witness a weakening of democratic institutions across much of the Western world. The USA, which for much of the 20th century was held up as a beacon of democracy, now faces deep political polarisation and a growing distrust in its institutions. Political gridlock has become the norm, and the very framework of its democratic system, with its checks and balances, seems strained to breaking point. The UK has experienced its democratic crises, from the divisive Brexit referendum to ongoing concerns about transparency and integrity in government. Canada, traditionally seen as a bastion of political stability, has not been immune either, with rising populist movements and increasing scepticism about the efficacy of its parliamentary system. Western Europe, particularly in nations such as France and Italy, has seen the rise of anti-establishment parties that challenge the very principles of post-war European unity.

In both ancient Rome and the modern West, the decay of political institutions is not an isolated phenomenon. It is both a symptom and a cause of deeper societal issues. The distrust in governance, combined with a perception that the elite are disconnected from the concerns of the broader population, leads to a fragmentation of society. This societal fragmentation, as I will discuss, has far-reaching implications, contributing to civil unrest and the rise of authoritarian tendencies as people seek alternative forms of stability.

Societal Fragmentation

Rome was once a cohesive force, a vast empire united under a single political and legal system, bound together by a shared sense of Roman identity. Yet, as the centuries wore on, this sense of unity began to fray. The Empire's borders had expanded so far that maintaining a common cultural or political identity across its territories became increasingly difficult. The vast differences in language, religion, and local customs across the Empire's regions contributed to its eventual fragmentation. At the same time, within Rome itself, the gap between the wealthy elite and the common people widened. Civil unrest and class warfare became more frequent, as the masses felt increasingly disenfranchised by the patrician class that dominated Roman politics and society.

In our present era, societal fragmentation is a growing concern throughout much of the Western world. The post-World War II period was marked by a sense of unity, with shared democratic values and common goals guiding much of the West's development. However, this unity is fraying. In the USA, political polarisation has reached unprecedented levels, with left and right-wing factions seemingly unable to agree on even the most basic tenets of governance. The societal divide has spilt over into violent protests, mass shootings, and an overall sense of instability. The UK, too, has seen its fair share of societal fragmentation, with the Brexit vote revealing deep divides not just between political factions but also between generations, regions, and social classes.

Canada and Western Europe are facing similar challenges. In Canada, debates over Indigenous rights, immigration, and economic inequality have brought to the fore long-standing issues that had been simmering under the surface. In Western Europe, the refugee crisis, combined with economic disparities between member states of the European Union, has led to a rise in nationalism and Euroscepticism, further fragmenting the social fabric.

Much like Rome, we are witnessing the weakening of the bonds that once held our societies together. The concept of a shared national identity, which in the post-war era was central to the West's stability, is being challenged by the forces of globalisation, immigration, and economic inequality. Without a concerted effort to rebuild a sense of common purpose, this fragmentation could lead to a further breakdown in the social order, just as it did in Rome.

Military Overextension and Global Overreach

One of the key factors that contributed to Rome's decline was its military overextension. At its height, the Roman Empire stretched across three continents, with a vast military presence required to maintain control over its territories. This overextension placed enormous strain on the Empire's resources, both financial and human. The constant need for soldiers led to a reliance on mercenaries and non-Roman recruits, weakening the cohesion and loyalty within the military. As Rome's enemies grew bolder, the Empire found itself fighting on multiple fronts, unable to effectively defend its borders. This overreach ultimately contributed to the collapse of the Western Roman Empire, as barbarian invasions chipped away at its territories.

In the modern West, there are clear parallels in the form of global overreach. The USA, in particular, has maintained a sprawling network of military bases across the globe, and it has been involved in numerous conflicts over the past few decades. From the wars in Afghanistan and Iraq to the ongoing tensions in the Middle East, the USA has been engaged in costly military operations that have drained its resources and stretched its military thin. Similarly, the UK has been involved in military operations far beyond its borders, often as a close ally of the USA. Canada and Western Europe, while less militarily aggressive, are still part of NATO and have committed resources to various international conflicts.

This global overreach has placed a significant burden on the Western world's economies and societies. Defence spending continues to consume vast portions of national budgets, while domestic needs such as infrastructure, healthcare, and education often go underfunded. Moreover, just as Rome's reliance on mercenaries weakened its military, the modern West's reliance on military contractors and alliances with sometimes-questionable partners has led to a weakening of its moral authority and international standing.

Economic Stagnation and Inequality

The economic decline of Rome is another critical aspect of its fall. During its peak, the Roman economy was driven by a complex system of trade, taxation, and agriculture, which allowed it to fund its vast military and public works. However, as the Empire expanded, so too did the costs of maintaining its infrastructure and military. The heavy taxation required to fund these efforts led to widespread economic stagnation, as the lower classes found themselves unable to keep up with the rising costs of living. Inflation, currency devaluation, and a lack of economic innovation all contributed to Rome's eventual financial collapse.

Today, many Western nations are grappling with similar economic challenges. Economic inequality is on the rise, with the wealth gap between the richest and poorest in society widening at an alarming rate. In the USA, wealth concentration in the hands of a few has led to growing discontent among the lower and middle classes, with stagnant wages and rising living costs further exacerbating the problem. The UK has experienced a similar trend, with austerity measures and the aftermath of Brexit contributing to economic instability. In Canada and Western Europe, while the situation is somewhat less pronounced, there are still clear signs of economic stagnation and inequality, particularly in regions that have been left behind by globalisation.

The national debt is another key indicator of decline. The Roman Empire, by the time of its fall, was deeply indebted, with its once-great wealth drained by military campaigns, public works, and a bloated bureaucracy. In the modern West, national debt levels are at historic highs, with countries borrowing heavily to fund their military operations, social programmes, and economic stimulus measures. This debt burden poses a serious threat to long-term stability, as governments are forced to prioritise debt repayment over necessary investments in infrastructure, education, and social welfare.

The national debt is indeed one of the most telling indicators of a society in decline, a symptom of deeper systemic issues that can undermine the long-term stability of a nation. The comparison between the Roman Empire at its peak and the modern West is especially apt when we examine the parallels between the fiscal irresponsibility that plagued late Rome and the alarming debt levels of Western countries today. Both eras reveal a tendency to prioritise short-term solutions often in the form of debasing currency or borrowing massive sums of money over sustainable economic policies, and both ultimately face the consequences of these decisions.

In the latter stages of the Roman Empire, the state's finances were increasingly strained by the demands of military defence, the construction of public works, and the maintenance of a bloated bureaucracy. Initially, Rome had amassed immense wealth through conquests, trade, and taxation. However, as the Empire expanded, so did the costs of maintaining it. Military campaigns became increasingly expensive, especially as external threats from barbarian tribes grew more frequent and severe. Additionally, the empire's public works grandiose projects designed to display Rome's might and sophistication further drained the imperial treasury. Over time, these costs overwhelmed Rome's revenue streams, pushing the empire into debt.

To meet these expenses, Roman emperors resorted to debasing their currency. This was done by reducing the silver content of Roman coins, which allowed the state to produce more coins without acquiring more precious metals. While this provided a temporary solution to Rome's fiscal woes, it had long-term consequences for the economy. As the value of the coinage fell, inflation spiralled out of control. Roman citizens began to lose trust in the value of their currency, and the once-strong economic foundation of the empire started to crumble. By the 3rd century AD, the empire's currency had been so debased that it was virtually worthless, leading to economic stagnation, a collapse in trade, and widespread poverty. The decline of the Roman currency became a physical representation of the empire's weakening power and influence.

This pattern finds a stark parallel in the modern West, particularly when we examine the way Western governments manage national debt and money supply. Instead of debasing coinage, contemporary Western governments engage in what is essentially the modern equivalent: printing money through mechanisms like quantitative easing. Central banks, particularly in the United States, the United Kingdom, and the European Union, have increasingly resorted to creating money to fund government spending and stimulate economies, particularly in times of crisis, such as the 2008 financial collapse and the COVID-19 pandemic.

Quantitative easing (QE) involves central banks purchasing government bonds and other securities, effectively injecting new money into the economy. While this can provide short-term economic relief, as it did during the recent crises, it also leads to the devaluation of currency over time, much like Rome's debasement of silver coins. The supply of money increases without a corresponding increase in the underlying value of goods and services, leading to inflation and the erosion of purchasing power. As in Rome, this tactic undermines public confidence in the stability of the currency and leads to long-term economic instability. Inflation, particularly in the aftermath of QE policies, has been a growing concern in the West. Prices of essential goods have risen, wage stagnation has persisted, and the average citizen is finding it increasingly difficult to maintain their standard of living.

One of the most pressing issues in the modern West is the skyrocketing level of national debt. Western governments have, in recent decades, accumulated unprecedented levels of debt to finance a range of activities, from military operations abroad to expansive social programmes at home. In the United States, for instance, the national debt now exceeds $33 trillion, a figure that represents over 100% of the country's Gross Domestic Product (GDP). The United Kingdom, Canada, and many Western European nations face similarly unsustainable debt levels. These debts are primarily fuelled by borrowing to cover fiscal deficits, which occur when governments spend more than they collect in revenue. As a result, Western nations are increasingly reliant on borrowing to fund their military, public services, and social safety nets.

Much like in Rome, where military overextension strained the empire's finances, modern Western nations are also heavily burdened by the cost of maintaining global military influence. The United States, for instance, spends over $800 billion annually on defence, maintaining bases in countries around the world and funding conflicts that, in many cases, have no clear end. The UK, too, has historically maintained a costly global military presence, although on a smaller scale. As these military commitments continue to drain national resources, governments find themselves in a precarious situation: prioritising military expenditure while struggling to invest adequately in critical domestic infrastructure, education, healthcare, and social welfare.

In Rome, military spending was similarly unsustainable. As the empire expanded, the costs of defending its vast borders increased dramatically. By the 4th and 5th centuries, Rome faced a growing number of external threats from barbarian groups, and the empire's military had become reliant on expensive mercenaries. These mercenaries were often paid in the increasingly worthless Roman currency, which led to further discontent and a weakened military. As the financial burdens of maintaining the empire grew, the Roman state became increasingly indebted, unable to cover the costs of its defence. Ultimately, Rome's inability to fund its military efforts contributed to its vulnerability to external invasions, particularly from the Visigoths, Vandals, and other groups that eventually sacked the Empire.

Another similarity between Rome and the modern West is the role that social programmes and public spending play in driving debt. In late Rome, a bloated bureaucracy and the maintenance of a vast welfare state placed enormous financial pressure on the Empire. Public grain distributions, known as *Annona*, were provided to the urban poor, and the Empire also funded elaborate public entertainments, such as gladiatorial games, in an attempt to pacify the masses. These programmes, while popular with the people, placed immense strain on the imperial treasury, particularly as the economy began to falter. To placate an increasingly restless population, the Roman state expanded these welfare programmes, exacerbating its fiscal crisis.

Today, the modern welfare state has similarly ballooned in many Western countries. Social programmes, including pensions, healthcare, unemployment benefits, and housing assistance, are essential to the social fabric of Western democracies, but they are also costly. In countries such as the United States, the UK, and much of Western Europe, government spending on social programmes continues to rise, often funded by borrowing rather than by sustainable taxation. This has led to growing national debts, which in turn require increasing interest payments. As more government revenue is diverted to servicing debt, there is less available for investments in critical areas like infrastructure, education, and innovation. This vicious cycle of borrowing, spending, and debt repayment mirrors the Roman Empire's financial decline, as more and more of the state's resources were consumed by efforts to manage its debt and fund unsustainable public programmes.

Moreover, the consequences of this debt burden extend beyond the economic sphere. In both late Rome and the modern West, excessive debt weakens the state's capacity to respond effectively to crises. Just as Rome found itself unable to muster the resources necessary to fend off invasions or rebuild after internal crises, today's Western nations are similarly constrained by their debt. In the event of another major financial crisis, or a geopolitical conflict requiring significant military expenditure, Western governments may find themselves unable to borrow further or to print more money without triggering runaway inflation.

The lessons from Rome's financial mismanagement are clear. The practice of debasing currency to fund short-term needs ultimately led to the collapse of Rome's economy, and the modern West is at risk of a similar fate if current fiscal policies persist. While printing money and increasing national debt may provide temporary relief from economic challenges, the long-term consequences are far more damaging. As we have seen in both late Rome and today's Western economies, the accumulation of unsustainable debt leads to inflation, stagnation, and a weakening of national institutions.

The issue of national debt, as highlighted by the current fiscal projections in the US, Canada, the EU, and the UK, is not only a modern economic concern but also a significant historical parallel to the late Roman Empire. In both instances, unchecked spending, overextended commitments, and the mismanagement of fiscal policies have placed immense pressure on the sustainability of the state, with both societies prioritising short-term political and military objectives at the expense of long-term stability. The modern West's spiralling national debt, much like Rome's fiscal collapse, reflects a fundamental weakness in governance and economic foresight. Let us delve deeper into these comparisons to understand the consequences and potential outcomes of such financial irresponsibility.

The Roman Experience: Debt and Fiscal Mismanagement

By the late stages of the Roman Empire, the state's finances were in disarray. In earlier centuries, Rome's wealth had been bolstered by conquest, extensive trade, and a well-functioning system of taxation. However, as the empire expanded, the costs of maintaining its vast borders, funding the army, and constructing grand public works spiralled out of control. The Roman state was increasingly forced to rely on extraordinary measures to fund its operations, including heavy taxation, debasement of its currency (as discussed earlier), and borrowing. These measures undermined the stability of the empire's economy and placed Rome on a path towards insolvency.

In particular, the Roman government's reliance on borrowing was a key indicator of its inability to maintain fiscal discipline. While the empire initially borrowed to fund military campaigns and public infrastructure projects, these debts quickly ballooned as Rome struggled to meet its financial obligations. The increased cost of maintaining its far-flung territories and paying off foreign mercenaries further compounded this problem. Like the governments of today, Rome eventually found itself in a position where debt interest payments began to crowd out other vital expenditures, such as maintaining its army and supporting its infrastructure.

The US Debt Crisis: A Warning from History

The situation in the modern United States mirrors this troubling pattern. The projections for the US federal debt reaching historic highs over the next decade signal a dangerous trajectory. The recent projections indicate that the US debt-to-GDP ratio and interest payments will continue to rise, potentially reaching unsustainable levels by 2026-2027. One crucial point to understand here is that growth alone cannot solve this issue an unrealistic growth rate of 4% or more would be necessary to stabilise the debt without corrective fiscal measures, which is far beyond current projections. Moreover, the risk of a recession, as flagged in these analyses, looms large, further complicating the government's ability to manage its debt.

This brings us back to the Roman Empire, which also reached a point where no amount of economic growth or territorial expansion could offset the costs of maintaining the empire. Like Rome, the US has reached a stage where the sheer size of its debt places it in a precarious position. While Rome debased its currency to create more money, the US has engaged in massive borrowing, often funding its operations through deficit spending and, more recently, through policies like quantitative easing. The outcome is the same: inflation, public dissatisfaction, and a weakened economic foundation. In Rome's case, it was military overextension and political instability that eventually led to its collapse. For the US, while military spending remains a significant factor, it is the growing debt burden that threatens the integrity of the nation's economy and its ability to function as a global superpower.

Canada's Debt and the Cost of Social Programmes

Canada presents another instructive example of how the burden of national debt can undermine a nation's long-term stability. The Trudeau government's penchant for increasing taxes, spending, and borrowing has put the country on a path toward record deficits. In 2024/25 alone, federal programme spending is projected to reach $483.6 billion, with deficits exceeding $20 billion per year for the next four years. This increase in spending is driven in part by social programmes, a hallmark of the modern Canadian welfare state.

While these programmes are popular and essential to maintaining social harmony, they are being funded through borrowing rather than through sustainable fiscal policies. This is not unlike Rome's *annona* welfare system, which provided free or heavily subsidised grain to Roman citizens to ensure political stability. Over time, however, this practice became a financial burden that the Roman state could no longer afford. As Rome's economy weakened, the ability to provide for its citizens through welfare diminished, leading to widespread discontent and social unrest.

Canada's approach to managing its national debt poses a similar risk. As interest payments on debt begin to take up a larger share of government revenue, there will be less money available for social programmes, infrastructure investment, and other critical areas. Just as Rome eventually had to choose between funding its military or maintaining its welfare system, Canada may soon face hard choices about where to allocate its limited resources. The increase in the capital gains inclusion rate, a measure meant to raise additional revenue, will likely deter investment at a time when Canada's economy needs growth. This, too, mirrors Rome's experience, as increasingly desperate attempts to raise revenue through taxation and currency manipulation ultimately stifled economic productivity.

Europe's Debt Dilemma: Echoes of Roman Disintegration

The European Union also faces significant fiscal challenges, with many member states grappling with higher debt levels and increasing interest rates. The pandemic, followed by the economic fallout from Russia's invasion of Ukraine, has placed additional pressure on EU economies. Long-term projections suggest that many EU countries will need to make substantial fiscal adjustments to reduce their debt-to-GDP ratios. Some will need to raise their primary balances by more than 2% of GDP to achieve debt-reducing targets. This is a significant burden that echoes the challenges faced by the later Roman

Empire, which struggled to find the resources needed to manage its sprawling territories and pay its ever-growing debts.

Just as the Roman Empire was divided into the Eastern and Western Roman Empires, with the West ultimately collapsing under the weight of its financial and military burdens, there is a risk that modern Europe could see increasing fragmentation as wealthier nations distance themselves from those with greater debt. Countries like Germany and the Netherlands, which have more fiscal space, may be able to manage the challenges posed by higher debt and interest rates. However, nations like Italy, Spain, and Greece, with higher debt burdens and fewer resources, may struggle to maintain their financial stability. The collapse of trust between the richer and poorer provinces of the Roman Empire contributed to its disintegration, and the same could happen in the EU if wealthier member states become unwilling to subsidise the poorer ones.

The UK: Deficit Spending and Borrowing

The situation in the UK, where government borrowing reached £120 billion in 2023/24, further exemplifies the dangerous path of deficit spending. Government revenue was £1.1 trillion, while spending was £1.2 trillion, leaving a deficit equivalent to 4.4% of GDP. This deficit, while not as large as some of the worst years in post-war Britain, is still a clear sign of a government living beyond its means. Borrowing of £120 billion is equivalent to around £1,780 per head of the UK population, a figure that highlights just how much of the burden will fall on future generations.

The UK's predicament can be compared to the Roman Empire's later years when Roman emperors resorted to increasingly desperate measures to fund their operations. Just as Rome's citizens bore the brunt of higher taxes and reduced public services, British taxpayers will ultimately pay for today's borrowing through higher taxes, inflation, or reduced government spending. Without a clear plan to return to a balanced budget, the UK risks falling into the same trap as Rome where short-term political considerations take precedence over long-term fiscal responsibility.

The Consequences of Inaction

The common thread that links the fiscal crises of Rome and the modern West is the failure of political leaders to address the underlying issues of unsustainable spending, borrowing, and overextension. In Rome, these problems led to the eventual collapse of the Western Empire, as it was no longer able to fund its military or maintain the trust of its citizens. In the modern West, the consequences of continued fiscal irresponsibility could be just as dire. If countries like the US, Canada, and the UK do not take steps to reduce their national debt and return to balanced budgets, they may face inflation, stagnation, and an eventual loss of international influence.

Moreover, the rising cost of servicing debt limits the ability of governments to invest in critical areas like infrastructure, education, and healthcare. Just as Rome neglected its internal infrastructure in favour of military spending, the modern West risks falling behind in areas that are essential to long-term economic growth and stability. If Western nations continue down this path, they could face a future where debt repayments take up an ever-larger share of government revenue, leaving little room for the kinds of investments that would enable future generations to prosper.

Lessons from Rome

The lessons from Rome are clear: excessive borrowing, combined with fiscal mismanagement and political short-sightedness, can bring even the most powerful of empires to its knees. The modern West, much like the late Roman Empire, is grappling with unsustainable debt levels, a growing reliance on borrowing, and political leaders who are reluctant to make the hard decisions necessary to secure long-term stability. If the West does not heed the warnings of history, it may find itself facing the same fate as Rome a gradual but inevitable decline, driven by the very fiscal irresponsibility that once seemed like a solution to short-term problems.

If the West does not heed the warnings of history, it could follow the same path as Rome, facing economic collapse and a loss of global influence as a result of its inability to manage its finances responsibly. The parallels between Rome's debased coinage and the West's overreliance on debt and money printing are stark reminders that fiscal irresponsibility has always been a key driver of decline. As Rome faltered under the weight of its financial mismanagement, so too might the West, unless it takes bold steps to address its growing debt crisis and rein in the excesses of short-term economic policies.

Civil Unrest and Diminishing Influence

Finally, one of the most visible signs of Rome's decline was the civil unrest that plagued the Empire in its later years. From the infamous "Crisis of the Third Century" to the numerous internal revolts, Rome struggled to maintain order as its citizens grew increasingly disillusioned with their leaders. This unrest was both a cause and a consequence of the Empire's weakening power, as internal strife made it easier for external enemies to exploit Rome's vulnerabilities.

In today's Western world, we are witnessing a rise in civil unrest, with protests, riots, and social movements becoming more frequent and more intense. The USA, in particular, has seen significant civil unrest in recent years, with movements such as Black Lives Matter and various right-wing militia groups challenging the status quo. The UK has experienced its share of unrest, particularly in the aftermath of Brexit and during protests over economic inequality. Canada, though often perceived as a peaceful nation, has seen rising tensions over indigenous rights and environmental concerns. In Western Europe, protests against austerity measures, immigration policies, and the perceived failures of the European Union have led to widespread unrest in countries such as France, Italy, and Spain.

The rise in civil unrest in today's Western world is not merely the product of spontaneous movements but is being driven by deliberate efforts to destabilise society. Groups such as ANTIFA, climate activists, and various far-left factions have gained significant traction, actively working towards the disruption of established social and political systems. Many of these groups, often backed by influential financiers like George Soros, promote radical ideologies that challenge the very foundations of Western society, much like the internal actors who contributed to the destabilisation of the Roman Empire during its decline.

ANTIFA, a loosely organised group that operates under the banner of anti-fascism, has been at the forefront of violent protests and demonstrations, particularly in the United States and parts of Europe. While they claim to be fighting against authoritarianism and right-wing extremism, their methods frequently involve violent confrontations with law enforcement, vandalism, and the disruption of civil order. These actions, often coordinated and funded by shadowy organisations, parallel the rise of extremist factions in Rome that sought to challenge the imperial order through violence and disruption. Just as in Rome, where political factions and armed groups increasingly fought for control and dominance, today's anarchist and far-left movements similarly seek to dismantle existing structures of governance through chaos and disorder.

Moreover, the role of climate activists, many of whom are also linked to left-wing movements, has become increasingly politicised. While environmental concerns are undoubtedly important, the methods employed by some of these groups including blockading infrastructure, disrupting commerce, and engaging in acts of civil disobedience have contributed to a growing sense of instability. The funding behind some of these activists, often traced back to individuals like Soros, raises concerns about whether these movements are genuinely grassroots or part of a broader effort to weaken societal cohesion. Rome, too, saw a decline in social stability when various groups, often with external backing or political motivations, began to challenge the status quo, leading to increased division and conflict within the Empire.

The modern-day immigration policies, heavily promoted by left-wing and socialist factions in Western Europe, the UK, and North America, also contribute to societal breakdown. While these policies are often framed as humanitarian efforts, they have led to mass immigration on a scale that many argue is unsustainable. This has resulted in growing tensions between immigrant communities and native populations, exacerbating economic disparities, and straining public services. In the Roman Empire, similar patterns emerged as Rome struggled to integrate the large numbers of non-Roman peoples who had settled within its borders. Over time, these groups, often with little allegiance to the Roman state, contributed to the weakening of Rome's internal cohesion, as ethnic and cultural tensions mounted. The modern West, like late Rome, faces the challenge of maintaining social order in the face of demographic and cultural shifts that threaten to overwhelm the institutions meant to preserve stability.

The issue of mass migration into the West is not just a humanitarian matter but a political and economic strategy, often employed by elites and politicians for their gain. This pattern echoes the decline of the Roman Empire, where similar manipulations of migration for short-term advantage led to long-term destabilisation. In my previous book, *Influx*, I explored this dynamic in detail, tracing how the political exploitation of mass migration has become one of the most pressing challenges for modern Western societies. This phenomenon, when examined alongside the experiences of Rome, highlights how migration can be weaponised by those in power to serve their interests, even at the expense of national stability and cohesion.

In today's Western world, immigration policies often framed as compassionate and inclusive are frequently promoted by left-wing and socialist factions. While humanitarian rhetoric is employed to justify these policies, the underlying motivations often involve political or financial benefits for elites. Politicians may seek to expand their voter bases by appealing to immigrant populations or leveraging the availability of cheap labour to satisfy corporate interests. Mass immigration, particularly from regions where cultural and religious values sharply contrast with those of the West, has created deep divisions within host nations. Many of these immigrants come from societies with religious doctrines, particularly Islamic teachings, that are often inimical to Western liberal values such as secularism, gender equality, and freedom of speech. Rather than integrating into the host societies, a significant portion of these migrant populations maintain strong cultural ties to their countries of origin, and in some cases, their values are in direct conflict with those of the West. This refusal to assimilate creates parallel societies, undermining social cohesion and heightening tensions between native populations and immigrant communities.

In this context, it is important to consider how these immigration policies are often used by political elites to their advantage. By supporting large-scale migration, politicians can claim the moral high ground, portraying themselves as champions of diversity and human rights. However, the costs of these policies are disproportionately borne by the working and middle classes, who see their job opportunities shrink, wages stagnate, and public services become overwhelmed. The elites, on the other hand, benefit from the influx of cheap labour and the political capital gained from portraying their actions as altruistic. This dynamic mirrors the exploitation of immigration by the Roman elites, who similarly manipulated tribal movements for their own political and economic advantage.

During Rome's decline, the elites and senators were often complicit in allowing large-scale migrations of tribal peoples, such as the Goths, Vandals, and other groups, into Roman territories. These movements were frequently motivated by short-term gains, whether it was securing military alliances, increasing tax revenues, or providing a source of cheap labour for Roman estates. However, these migrants were often not fully integrated into Roman society, either by choice or due to a lack of effort from the Roman state. Instead, many of these groups maintained their tribal identities and allegiances, with little loyalty to Rome itself. Over time, this contributed to internal fractures within the Empire, as these non-Roman groups, culturally and ethnically distinct from the Roman populace, became a destabilising force. In some cases, these tribal groups were even manipulated by Roman elites as political tools, used to gain leverage over rivals in the Senate or to challenge the authority of the emperor. This cynical use of migration for political advantage ultimately weakened Rome from within, as the Empire became increasingly fragmented along ethnic and cultural lines.

Today, we see similar patterns of fragmentation across much of the West. In the UK, for instance, mass immigration has led to the creation of ethnic enclaves in cities like London, Birmingham, and Manchester, where immigrant populations are concentrated, often with little interaction with the broader British society. The same can be seen in France, with its *banlieues*, where large immigrant populations, many of whom are Muslim, live in isolation from the mainstream French population. This separation has led to significant cultural and religious tensions, particularly as these communities often hold values that conflict with France's secular principles. Canada and parts of Western Europe face similar challenges, as immigrant communities with strong cultural identities resist assimilation, creating tensions with the native populations. This division is further exacerbated by political elites who, rather than addressing the growing sense of discontent among native citizens, continue to push for even more lenient immigration policies.

The Roman experience provides a stark warning for the modern West. Rome's inability to control and integrate the large numbers of migrants and tribal peoples within its borders led to a breakdown in social cohesion, much as we are seeing today in Western societies. Just as Rome allowed its borders to be overrun by groups who had little allegiance to the Roman state, the modern West has allowed large-scale immigration by groups who often have little interest in adopting the values and norms of their host nations. This failure to assimilate migrants not only erodes national identity but also weakens the institutions that have traditionally upheld the stability of Western societies.

In both cases, the motivations for allowing these migrations were largely self-serving. Rome's elites, much like today's politicians, saw immigration as a means to an end whether it was securing political power, increasing wealth, or providing a source of labour. However, the long-term consequences of these policies were disastrous. The lack of integration and the rise of parallel societies contributed to the eventual collapse of the Roman Empire, as the internal divisions created by mass migration made it easier for external enemies to exploit Rome's vulnerabilities. Similarly, the West today faces the risk of fragmentation as mass migration continues to strain public services, exacerbate economic inequalities, and create cultural conflicts within societies that were once relatively homogeneous.

The influx of migrants, many of whom follow a religion that is often at odds with Western values, presents a particularly significant challenge. The refusal of many immigrant groups to assimilate into Western culture is not just a matter of cultural difference; it is a direct threat to the social cohesion that has long underpinned the success of Western democracies. Just as Rome struggled to maintain its identity in the face of large-scale migrations, the West today is grappling with a similar crisis of identity. If left unchecked, the continued influx of migrants who refuse to integrate and the political manipulation of immigration for short-term gain could lead to the same kind of societal breakdown that ultimately contributed to the fall of Rome.

In one of my earlier books, *Influx*, I explored how modern mass migration, driven by both political and economic forces, is reshaping the social, political, and economic landscape of the West. The parallels with Rome's decline are striking. Just as Rome's elites allowed tribal movements to serve their interests, today's political class uses immigration as a tool for political advantage, often at the expense of national unity and stability. If the West does not learn from the mistakes of Rome, it too could find itself facing a similar fate, as unchecked immigration continues to erode the very foundations of Western society.

Just as Rome saw internal decay fuelled by competing factions, corrupt officials, and external pressures, today's Western societies are grappling with movements that seek to radically alter the fabric of their nations. The breakdown of Roman society was not just the result of external invasions but also the culmination of years of internal fragmentation, driven by competing interests and a failure to maintain a cohesive identity. We, too, are at risk of a similar fate if the forces seeking to destabilise Western society are not countered.

The political and social unrest that we see today whether through anarchist movements like ANTIFA, climate radicalism, or unchecked immigration policies driven by left-wing factions reflects a deeper crisis in the West. Coupled with this internal unrest is a diminishing influence on the world stage. Just as Rome's power waned in its later years, the modern West is seeing its dominance challenged by rising powers such as China, Russia, and India.

Just as Rome's inability to control its internal divisions ultimately led to its collapse, the modern West faces a similar threat if we do not take steps to address the forces that are actively working to undermine the stability and integrity of our societies.

Chapter 3: Economic Stagnation and the Collapse of Infrastructure

Throughout history, the decline of great civilisations has often been marked by a distinct and troubling pattern: economic stagnation coupled with the collapse of infrastructure. The Roman Empire, once the beacon of prosperity and innovation, found itself ensnared in such a fate. As I explore in the earlier chapters, Rome at its zenith showcased remarkable economic strength, military might, and cultural dominance, much like the modern West in the post-World War II era. Yet, just as the cracks began to show in Rome's once unshakeable foundation, we now witness unsettling parallels in Western society. The question remains: are we witnessing the beginning of a similar collapse?

The Economic Breakdown in the Roman Empire

To truly understand the depth of Rome's decline, we must first examine the economic factors that contributed to its downfall. During the height of the Empire, Rome was an economic powerhouse, controlling vast territories that stretched across three continents. Trade routes spanned from the East to the farthest reaches of Britannia, bringing goods, wealth, and culture. However, as the Empire expanded, so did the costs of maintaining its vast infrastructure and military presence.

Inflation became one of the earliest signs of economic decay in Rome. The devaluation of the currency, particularly the silver denarius, began under Emperor Nero in the mid-1st century AD. By reducing the silver content in coins to fund the ever-growing needs of the state, Rome effectively initiated a long-term inflationary crisis. Over time, the value of the denarius plummeted, leading to a loss of confidence in Roman currency and rampant inflation. Citizens found their savings eroded, and trade became increasingly difficult as prices for goods skyrocketed.

Taxation, while essential for maintaining state power and public services, has historically been a double-edged sword. In the Roman Empire, as I discussed in earlier sections, taxation played a critical role in both the rise and eventual decline of the state. Initially, taxes were levied to strengthen the Empire, funding its military campaigns, infrastructure projects, and public welfare programmes, such as the *cura annonae*, the grain dole that kept Roman citizens fed. However, as the Empire began to weaken, this once-valuable tool became a source of instability and decay, particularly for the provinces and the poorest citizens.

The West today, particularly the United States, the United Kingdom, and Western Europe, faces a similar predicament. While taxation remains a vital means of sustaining public services, infrastructure, and social welfare, it is also increasingly seen as burdensome by large segments of society. The lessons from Rome's collapse are stark: when taxation is not applied equitably or is perceived as oppressive, it can erode the very economic base on which a state relies.

Rome's Taxation Crisis: From Strength to Exploitation

During its height, Rome's taxation system was relatively balanced. Citizens of the Roman heartland were taxed relatively lightly, while the provinces bore the bulk of the financial burden. Taxes were used to fund the massive Roman military apparatus, infrastructure projects like roads and aqueducts, and public services such as the grain dole, which helped maintain social order. However, as the Empire expanded, the cost of maintaining such vast territories grew disproportionately. Military expenditures ballooned, especially as Rome faced increasing pressure from external threats like the Germanic tribes and the Sassanid Empire.

To meet these growing demands, successive emperors increased taxes, particularly in the provinces. This led to the creation of a more complex and decentralised system of local taxation, which eventually became a breeding ground for corruption. Tax collectors, or *publicani*, were often private contractors who purchased the right to collect taxes from the state. Their profits came from whatever they could collect over and above the amount owed to the government. This system, known as *tax farming*, led to widespread abuse. Tax collectors frequently inflated assessments and extorted the local population, often pushing poorer citizens into poverty. In extreme cases, entire villages were abandoned as people fled their homes to escape the crushing tax burden.

The result was a self-perpetuating cycle of economic stagnation. As citizens and small landowners were driven from their homes, agricultural production the backbone of the Roman economy declined. Wealthy landowners, who were more capable of evading taxes or negotiating favourable terms with corrupt officials, amassed more land. This concentration of wealth further exacerbated economic inequality, while the tax base continued to shrink, leaving the Empire unable to meet its growing financial obligations.

In many ways, Rome's taxation system became self-destructive. The very tool that was supposed to sustain the Empire instead strangled it, eroding the economic vitality of the provinces and contributing to social unrest. As the system became increasingly corrupt and inefficient, the Roman state found itself unable to maintain the infrastructure and military forces necessary to defend its borders.

Modern Parallels: Taxation and Inequality in the West

In the modern West, taxation remains a key mechanism for funding public services, infrastructure, and social safety nets. However, just as in Rome, it has become a source of growing dissatisfaction, particularly as economic inequality widens. In the United States, for instance, the tax system is often criticised for favouring the wealthy and corporations, while placing a disproportionate burden on the middle class and the poor. This is evident in the regressive nature of certain taxes, such as payroll taxes, which affect lower-income workers more than the wealthy.

The US tax system is highly complex, with numerous loopholes and deductions that allow corporations and high-net-worth individuals to reduce their tax liabilities significantly. As a result, the wealthiest individuals and corporations often pay far less in taxes as a percentage of their income than ordinary citizens. According to data from the IRS, the effective tax rate for the top 1% of earners has fallen steadily over the past few decades, while the tax burden on middle-income families has remained relatively constant. This growing disparity has led to a perception that the system is fundamentally unfair a sentiment that echoes the discontent felt by the provinces in late Roman times, where the wealthy could often negotiate their tax obligations or evade them entirely.

In the UK and much of Western Europe, the situation is similar. While the tax systems in these countries tend to be more progressive than in the US, austerity measures following the 2008 financial crisis have disproportionately affected lower-income citizens. Public services have been cut, and taxes such as VAT (Value Added Tax) and other consumption taxes have been increased, which tend to hit poorer households harder than wealthier ones. Meanwhile, multinational corporations, particularly tech giants like Google, Amazon, and Apple, have been accused of using loopholes to avoid paying their fair share of taxes in these countries. This has sparked widespread outrage and calls for reform, yet significant action has been slow to materialise.

Just as in Rome, modern taxation policies in the West are contributing to economic inequality and social discontent. The concentration of wealth in the hands of a few, combined with a perception that the tax system is rigged against ordinary citizens, has led to growing resentment. In the US, movements like Occupy Wall Street and the resurgence of populism on both the left and right are, in part, responses to this perceived inequality. Similarly, in the UK, the

Brexit vote can be seen as a rejection of the political and economic status quo, driven by a sense that ordinary people were being left behind while the wealthy and powerful prospered.

Corruption and Evasion: The Modern *Publicani*

Another troubling parallel between the Roman Empire and the modern West is the role of corruption and tax evasion. In Rome, the *publicani* became notorious for their exploitative practices, enriching themselves at the expense of the state and the people. In much the same way, modern tax evasion and avoidance schemes have become rampant, particularly among corporations and the wealthy elite.

In the United States, it is estimated that tax evasion costs the government hundreds of billions of dollars each year. Much of this evasion is concentrated among the wealthy, who can afford to hire teams of lawyers and accountants to exploit loopholes in the tax code. Similarly, in the UK and Western Europe, the use of offshore tax havens has allowed corporations and individuals to shield vast amounts of wealth from taxation. The Panama Papers and Paradise Papers leaks revealed the extent of this practice, exposing how the global elite have used secretive financial structures to avoid paying taxes in their home countries.

The consequences of this tax evasion are profound. Just as in Rome, where the corruption of the *publicani* undermined the state's ability to collect revenue, modern tax avoidance and evasion erode the ability of governments to fund public services and infrastructure. This, in turn, exacerbates inequality and undermines social cohesion. When ordinary citizens feel that the wealthy are not paying their fair share, it breeds resentment and distrust in government a dynamic that was all too familiar in the later years of the Roman Empire.

The Self-Destructive Cycle of Taxation and Economic Instability

In Rome, the heavy tax burden on the provinces, combined with widespread corruption and inefficiency, created a vicious cycle of economic decline. As the provinces became poorer, the tax base shrank, forcing the state to raise taxes even further, which only worsened the situation. Over time, this self-destructive cycle contributed to the collapse of the Roman economy, and ultimately, the Empire itself.

The modern West risks falling into a similar trap. The growing concentration of wealth at the top, combined with tax policies that favour the wealthy, is eroding the economic base on which the state relies. As inequality rises and public services deteriorate, there is a growing sense of dissatisfaction and instability. Governments, facing increasing pressure to balance their budgets, often resort to austerity measures or regressive taxes, which only deepen the divide between the rich and the poor.

Furthermore, the growing reliance on debt to finance government expenditures, particularly in the United States parallels Rome's increasing reliance on extraordinary means, such as the debasement of currency, to meet its financial obligations. In both cases, these short-term solutions have long-term consequences. Just as Rome's debasement of the denarius contributed to inflation and economic instability, the modern West's growing debt burden posed a significant risk to long-term financial stability.

Learning from Rome: The Path Forward

The decline of Rome's taxation system offers valuable lessons for the modern West. First and foremost, taxation must be fair and equitable. When the burden of taxes falls disproportionately on the poor, as it did in Rome, it undermines the economic base and breeds social unrest. Similarly, when the wealthy can evade taxes or manipulate the system to their advantage, it erodes trust in government and weakens the state's ability to function effectively.

Reforming the tax systems in the modern West will require a commitment to equity and transparency. Closing loopholes that allow the wealthy to avoid taxes, increasing the progressivity of the tax code, and ensuring that corporations pay their fair share are essential steps to restoring trust and stability. Moreover, governments must resist the temptation to rely on short-term fixes, such as austerity measures or debt financing, which only exacerbate inequality and economic instability in the long run.

The lessons of Rome are clear: a state that cannot effectively and fairly collect taxes is a state that is destined to decline. Just as Rome's self-destructive tax policies contributed to its fall, the modern West risks a similar fate if it does not address the growing inequality and inefficiency in its taxation systems. The path forward will not be easy, but by learning from the mistakes of the past, we can work towards a more just and stable economic future.

Trade was the cornerstone of the Roman Empire's wealth and power, enabling the vast exchange of goods, culture, and ideas across the Mediterranean and beyond. It fuelled Rome's cities, supported its military, and connected far-flung provinces in a unified economic system. However, as the Empire began to crumble, the trade networks that once sustained this immense political and economic structure deteriorated. Banditry, piracy, and the rise of rival powers like the Sassanid Empire weakened these connections, plunging Rome into increasing isolation.

The decline of trade in the later Roman Empire provides a stark warning for the modern West. While the global economy today is vastly more interconnected through advanced technologies and institutions, the same vulnerabilities political instability, security threats, and the rise of economic rivals pose significant challenges. The slow collapse of Rome's trade networks and the resulting economic isolation find parallels in the growing strain on modern globalisation, where supply chains are becoming more fragile, trade is increasingly politicised, and geopolitical tensions threaten the smooth flow of goods and services. By comparing these two worlds, it becomes clear how vital trade is to the stability of civilisation and how dangerous it can be to neglect its maintenance.

The Roman Trade Network: Lifeblood of the Empire

During its height, Rome's economy was deeply reliant on a vast and intricate network of trade routes that spanned the Mediterranean and beyond. Goods such as grain from Egypt, spices from India, silk from China, and minerals from Spain flowed into the Empire, enriching its cities and fuelling its military machine. The Mediterranean Sea, often referred to as "Mare Nostrum" or "Our Sea" by the Romans, was at the heart of this system, facilitating the movement of goods from the farthest reaches of the Empire to the capital itself.

Rome's trade dominance was underpinned by two key factors: its military strength and its political stability. The legions ensured the safety of land and sea routes, while the efficient governance of the provinces allowed for smooth commercial exchanges. Rome's infrastructure, particularly its roads, ports, and aqueducts, also played a critical role in supporting trade. This interconnectedness allowed the Empire to amass incredible wealth and provided a degree of resilience against localised economic crises.

However, as the Empire entered its period of decline, these key pillars of Roman trade began to erode. Political instability, military overextension, and a weakening administrative apparatus made it increasingly difficult for Rome to maintain control over its trade networks. This loss of control had devastating consequences, not only for Rome's economy but for its society as a whole.

Political and Military Instability: The Collapse of Roman Trade

The decline of Rome's political and military power played a significant role in the collapse of its trade networks. As Rome faced internal strife such as political corruption, civil wars, and a weakening central authority it became less able to protect its trade routes. In particular, the Mediterranean Sea, once a secure highway for Roman merchants, became increasingly dangerous as piracy and banditry grew more common. Without the protection of the Roman navy and the legions, merchants were unwilling to risk their goods, leading to a significant decline in trade.

At the same time, Rome's overextension militarily meant that it could no longer defend its borders effectively. The Empire's northern provinces were constantly under threat from barbarian invasions, while the eastern provinces faced increasing pressure from the Sassanid Empire. These military challenges further disrupted trade, as once-thriving provinces like Gaul and Syria found themselves cut off from the broader Roman economy. The fragmentation of the Empire's political and military power, therefore, directly contributed to the collapse of its trade networks.

Similarly, in the modern West, political instability and military entanglements pose a significant threat to global trade. The 21st century has seen increasing political polarisation, economic nationalism, and regional conflicts that threaten the integrity of global supply chains. The United States, once the unchallenged leader of the global economic order, has become more inward-focused, questioning long-standing trade agreements and alliances. The UK, with its departure from the European Union through Brexit, has introduced new uncertainties into its trade relationships. Meanwhile, rising powers like China challenged Western dominance in global trade, much like the Sassanid Empire did to Rome.

The global economy is highly interdependent, with supply chains crisscrossing the globe to deliver goods in a timely and cost-efficient manner. However, this interdependence also creates vulnerabilities. Disruptions in one part of the world can quickly cascade throughout the system, as demonstrated by the COVID-19 pandemic, which exposed the fragility of global supply chains. Political instability, trade wars, and regional conflicts can have similarly destabilising effects. Just as Rome's loss of control over its trade routes contributed to its decline, modern Western economies must navigate these challenges to maintain their economic strength.

Banditry, Piracy, and the Breakdown of Trade Security

One of the most tangible manifestations of Rome's weakening grip on trade was the rise of banditry and piracy. As the Roman military became stretched too thin, it was no longer able to secure the sea lanes and highways that once made trade safe and reliable. Pirates began to plague the Mediterranean, disrupting maritime trade and making it difficult for merchants to transport goods between provinces. Overland routes were similarly affected, as banditry increased in regions like Gaul and North Africa. Merchants, fearing for their lives and their goods, began to limit their trade activities, further weakening the Empire's economy.

In the modern world, trade security remains a critical issue. While we no longer face the threat of pirates in the Mediterranean, the global economy is vulnerable to other forms of disruption, including cyberattacks, terrorism, and geopolitical tensions. Cyberattacks on critical infrastructure, such as ports or supply chain management systems, can cause massive disruptions to trade. Meanwhile, regional conflicts, such as the war in Ukraine, have shown how geopolitical instability can have ripple effects throughout the global economy, disrupting energy supplies, food production, and other key industries.

Furthermore, modern piracy, particularly off the coast of Somalia and in the South China Sea, still poses a threat to maritime trade. While the scale of piracy today is not comparable to that of late Rome, it serves as a reminder that even in the 21st century, the security of trade routes cannot be taken for granted. Just as Rome's inability to maintain control over its trade routes hastened its decline, modern Western economies must remain vigilant in ensuring the security of their supply chains.

Economic Isolation: Rome's Decline and the Rise of Rival Powers

As Rome's internal instability grew, its economic isolation deepened. Once the heart of a vast, interconnected economy, the

Roman Empire found itself increasingly cut off from the rest of the world. Trade with distant provinces and foreign powers slowed to a trickle, as merchants avoided the dangerous and unstable regions of the Empire. At the same time, rival powers like the Sassanid Empire in the East grew stronger, challenging Rome's dominance and offering alternative trade routes to regions like India and China.

Rome's economic isolation was further exacerbated by its failure to adapt to changing circumstances. As the Empire became more inward-focused, it failed to invest in new technologies or economic strategies that could have revitalised its trade networks. Instead, Rome clung to its old ways, even as the world around it changed. This failure to innovate and adapt contributed to the Empire's decline, as it became increasingly unable to compete with rising powers like the Sassanids and the emerging Islamic Caliphate.

The modern West faces similar challenges today. As globalisation has reshaped the world economy, Western powers like the United States and the European Union have found themselves facing increasing competition from rising powers, particularly China. China has positioned itself as a central hub of global trade, with its Belt and Road Initiative aiming to create new trade routes that bypass the traditional Western-dominated economic order. This mirrors the way the Sassanid Empire challenged Rome's dominance over trade with the East.

Moreover, the West's increasing reliance on complex global supply chains has created vulnerabilities. Disruptions to these supply chains, whether from geopolitical tensions, pandemics, or natural disasters, can have far-reaching consequences. The COVID-19 pandemic highlighted the fragility of these systems, as shortages of key goods like medical supplies and semiconductors reverberated throughout the global economy. Just as Rome found itself isolated and unable to sustain the trade networks that once supported its prosperity, the modern West must grapple with the risks of economic isolation and the need to diversify its trade relationships.

Globalisation, Technological Disruption, and Modern Economic Challenges

One of the defining features of the modern global economy is the unprecedented level of interconnectedness made possible by globalisation and technological innovation. The rise of global trade in the post-World War II era, combined with advances in transportation and communication technologies, has created an economic system that is far more integrated than anything Rome could have imagined. Yet, this interconnectedness has also brought new challenges.

Globalisation, much like Rome's vast trade networks, has lifted millions out of poverty and created immense wealth, particularly in the West. However, it has also led to rising inequality, as the benefits of global trade have been unevenly distributed. In many Western countries, manufacturing jobs have been outsourced to cheaper labour markets, hollowing out the middle class and leaving many workers without stable employment. This has led to growing discontent, particularly in regions that once thrived on industrial production.

Furthermore, technological disruption has created new challenges for the modern economy. The rise of automation, artificial intelligence, and digital platforms has transformed industries, leading to job displacement and economic uncertainty. While these technologies have the potential to drive economic growth, they also threaten to exacerbate inequality and destabilise traditional economic structures. In many ways, this mirrors the decline of Rome's economy, as the Empire failed to adapt to changing economic circumstances and new threats.

Modern Parallels: Rising Inequality, Inflation, and Stagnation

Today, we find unsettling echoes of Rome's economic woes in the modern West. In the United States, the United Kingdom, Canada, and across Western Europe, economies once hailed for their resilience and dynamism now face growing challenges. Rising inequality, inflationary pressures, and stagnation threaten to undermine the very fabric of these societies.

Since the global financial crisis of 2008, economic recovery in the West has been uneven at best. While stock markets have surged and corporate profits have reached new heights, wage growth has stagnated for many. Income inequality has reached levels not seen since the early 20th century. In the United States, the wealth gap between the richest and the poorest has continued to widen, with the top 1% controlling a staggering share of the nation's wealth. Similarly, in the United Kingdom, economic inequality remains a persistent problem, exacerbated by austerity measures and regional disparities.

Inflation, a problem Rome faced in its later years, has also reared its head once more in modern economies. The COVID-19 pandemic disrupted global supply chains, and the subsequent economic recovery has been marked by sharp inflationary pressures. The price of goods has risen significantly, and central banks have found themselves struggling to maintain control. As I discussed in Chapter 1, the evolution of modern economies from industrial powerhouses to service-based models has made them particularly vulnerable to such shocks. Unlike the Roman Empire, which devalued its currency to finance its ambitions, modern governments rely on complex monetary policy. Yet, the result is strikingly similar: ordinary citizens find their purchasing power eroding, while the wealthy remain insulated from the worst effects of inflation.

Stagnation, particularly in Western Europe, has become an entrenched issue. Many countries face sluggish growth, exacerbated by demographic changes and structural inefficiencies. In Italy, once the centre of the Roman Empire, GDP growth has remained anaemic for decades, while youth unemployment remains persistently high. Similarly, the UK and France, once leaders in innovation and industry, now find themselves grappling with ageing infrastructure and declining productivity.

The Collapse of Infrastructure: Rome's Decaying Roads, Bridges, and Aqueducts

Rome's greatness was not merely a result of its military conquests but also of its remarkable infrastructure. Roads, aqueducts, bridges, and public buildings represented the height of Roman engineering and facilitated the Empire's dominance. However, as the Empire weakened, so did its ability to maintain these critical systems. Roads that had once facilitated the rapid movement of armies and trade fell into disrepair, making it difficult to protect the Empire's farthest borders or ensure the flow of goods. Aqueducts, which had once provided a reliable supply of water to cities across the Empire, were left to deteriorate, leading to public health crises and further decline in urban centres.

The neglect of infrastructure was symptomatic of the broader decline in Roman governance and economic capacity. As corruption within the government became endemic, resources that should have been allocated to maintaining these vital systems were siphoned off by self-serving officials. The ability of the state to maintain its once-proud infrastructure eroded, and with it, so did the very foundation of the Roman economy and society.

Crumbling Infrastructure in the Modern West

In much the same way, the modern West faces an infrastructure crisis. Across the United States, bridges and roads are crumbling, water systems are outdated, and public transportation systems are often unreliable. The American Society of Civil Engineers has repeatedly given the country's infrastructure a poor rating, estimating that trillions of dollars in investment are needed to bring it up to an acceptable standard. In the UK, the situation is similar: ageing railways, neglected roads, and underfunded public services have become the norm.

The decline of infrastructure is not merely a matter of inconvenience; it is a direct threat to economic productivity and societal well-being. Just as in Rome, where the decay of roads and aqueducts contributed to the collapse of trade and public health, the deterioration of infrastructure in the modern West undermines the very systems that support economic growth. Businesses face higher transportation costs, public services are strained, and the quality of life for ordinary citizens deteriorates. Moreover, the political will to address these challenges often falters, with short-term political gains taking precedence over long-term investments in critical infrastructure.

Globalisation and Technological Disruption: A Double-Edged Sword

While Rome's decline was in part due to its inability to sustain its trade networks, the modern West faced a more complex set of challenges. Globalisation, which once promised unparalleled economic growth and integration, has proven to be a double-edged sword. While it has brought significant benefits, including lower costs for consumers and access to new markets, it has also contributed to the hollowing out of traditional industries in many Western countries.

The decline of manufacturing in the modern West, particularly in the United States and the United Kingdom, reflects an economic shift that is both emblematic of globalisation and reminiscent of the structural vulnerabilities that contributed to the fall of the Roman Empire. Once the backbone of these economies, manufacturing has been largely outsourced to lower-cost countries such as India, China, and Southeast Asia. This transformation has caused significant disruption in many Western nations, particularly in former industrial heartlands, where the loss of manufacturing jobs has led to economic stagnation, social unrest, and political polarization. Drawing comparisons between the industrial decline in the West and Rome's economic downturn offers valuable insights into the potential risks facing modern Western societies.

Manufacturing in the West: From Dominance to Decline

In the post-World War II era, manufacturing was the bedrock of the American and British economies, fuelling decades of prosperity and growth. The United States, with its vast industrial base, became the world's largest economy, producing goods ranging from automobiles to steel that were exported across the globe. Similarly, the United Kingdom, though diminished in its global empire, retained a strong manufacturing sector that was integral to its economy. The post-war boom in manufacturing created millions of well-paying jobs, established a strong middle class, and underpinned Western economic dominance.

However, by the late 20th century, this manufacturing supremacy began to erode. With the rise of globalisation, multinational corporations sought to lower production costs by outsourcing manufacturing to countries with cheaper labour markets, such as China, India, and Southeast Asia. These regions offered lower wages, fewer regulations, and access to growing consumer markets, making them attractive alternatives to Western manufacturing hubs. Consequently, industries that had once thrived in cities like Detroit, Sheffield, and Manchester began to decline, with factories closing and jobs disappearing.

This shift has had profound social and economic consequences. In many Western nations, particularly in the United States and the United Kingdom, former industrial regions have been left in a state of decay. The loss of manufacturing jobs has led to rising unemployment, economic stagnation, and a growing sense of disillusionment among the working class. Cities that were once the engines of national economies have become symbols of decline, struggling with poverty, crime, and political disenchantment. This economic hollowing out has contributed to the rise of populist political movements, which capitalise on the frustrations of those left behind by globalisation.

Outsourcing and the Roman Parallel: Economic Hollowing Out

The decline of manufacturing in the West mirrors, in some ways, the economic hollowing out that occurred in the later stages of the Roman Empire. While Rome did not have an industrial economy in the modern sense, it did rely on certain key economic sectors, such as agriculture, mining, and artisanal production, to sustain its wealth. In the early and middle periods of the Empire, Rome's economy was bolstered by a combination of conquest, slave labour, and efficient provincial administration, which allowed the Empire to extract wealth from its provinces and fund its infrastructure, military, and public works.

However, as the Empire expanded, the economic dynamics began to shift. The costs of maintaining a vast military presence across the provinces, coupled with increasing administrative inefficiency, placed a heavy strain on the economy. Much like the outsourcing of manufacturing in the modern West, Rome began to rely more heavily on the provinces to provide the economic sustenance needed to support the central Empire. Wealth and resources flowed increasingly from the periphery to the core, leading to economic stagnation in some provinces and growing inequality across the Empire.

One of the key parallels between Rome and the modern West is the issue of economic centralisation and the growing reliance on external sources of production. Just as the Roman Empire became dependent on its provinces for agricultural and material wealth, modern Western economies have outsourced much of their manufacturing to lower-cost countries. This reliance on external production creates vulnerabilities, as it exposes the core economy to external shocks, supply chain disruptions, and the economic policies of other nations. In the case of Rome, this economic over-reliance on the provinces made the Empire more susceptible to external pressures, such as invasions and trade disruptions. Similarly, the modern West's dependence on foreign manufacturing has created a new set of risks, particularly as geopolitical tensions rise.

The Impact of Outsourcing: Inequality, Social Unrest, and Political Fragmentation

One of the most significant consequences of outsourcing in the modern West has been the rise of inequality. The shift of manufacturing jobs to lower-cost countries has disproportionately affected working-class communities, particularly in regions that were once industrial strongholds. As factories have closed and jobs have disappeared, these regions have experienced economic decline, with fewer opportunities for well-paying employment. This has led to a widening gap between wealthy urban centres, which have benefitted from the globalisation of finance and technology, and economically depressed rural and industrial areas, where the effects of deindustrialisation are most acutely felt.

The Roman Empire experienced a similar rise in inequality in its later years. As the economic base of the Empire shifted, wealth became increasingly concentrated in the hands of a small elite, while the majority of the population struggled with poverty and insecurity. Large estates, or *latifundia*, came to dominate the agricultural landscape, driving small farmers out of business and creating a class of landless peasants. The economic disparities between the wealthy elite and the impoverished masses contributed to social unrest, civil wars, and a general sense of instability throughout the Empire.

In both the Roman and modern contexts, this growing inequality has had profound political consequences. In the late Roman Empire, the discontent among the lower classes, coupled with the increasing concentration of wealth and power among the elite, contributed to the weakening of political institutions and the rise of corruption. Similarly, in the modern West, the loss of manufacturing jobs and the resulting economic inequality have fuelled political polarisation and the rise of populist movements. Many voters in regions that have been left behind by globalisation feel alienated from the political and economic elite, leading to a growing distrust of democratic institutions and a sense of disillusionment with the political status quo.

The Consequences of Deindustrialisation: Infrastructure Decline and Economic Stagnation

In addition to the social and political consequences of outsourcing, the decline of manufacturing has also contributed to the deterioration of infrastructure in many Western countries. In the United States and the United Kingdom, for example, once-thriving industrial cities have seen their infrastructure roads, bridges, public transportation, and utilities fall into disrepair as local economies have stagnated. The loss of manufacturing jobs has led to a decline in tax revenues, making it more difficult for governments to invest in maintaining and upgrading infrastructure.

Rome, too, faced a similar problem in its later years. The collapse of trade networks and the economic stagnation of the provinces meant that the Empire was increasingly unable to maintain its vast infrastructure. Roads, aqueducts, and public buildings, which had once been the pride of Roman engineering, fell into disrepair. As trade declined and wealth was concentrated in fewer hands, the central government found it more difficult to finance large-scale public works, leading to a gradual decline in the quality of infrastructure across the Empire. The deterioration of infrastructure further weakened the Empire, as it became harder to transport goods, move armies, and maintain communication across the vast Roman territories.

In the modern West, the consequences of deindustrialisation have similarly contributed to the decline of infrastructure, particularly in regions that have been most affected by the loss of manufacturing jobs. The economic stagnation of former industrial heartlands has made it difficult for local governments to invest in the infrastructure needed to attract new businesses and create jobs. This, in turn, creates a vicious cycle of decline, as the lack of infrastructure investment further weakens the local economy, making it even harder for these regions to recover.

Globalisation and the Challenge of Economic Resilience

The outsourcing of manufacturing and the decline of industrial economies in the West can also be viewed as a symptom of broader challenges related to globalisation. While globalisation has brought significant benefits, such as lower consumer prices and access to new markets, it has also created new vulnerabilities. The global economy is now deeply interconnected, with supply chains stretching across continents and industries. This interconnectedness means that disruptions in one part of the world can quickly have ripple effects throughout the global economy.

In the case of manufacturing, the reliance on foreign production has exposed Western economies to the risks of supply chain disruptions, geopolitical tensions, and economic competition from rising powers like China and India. The COVID-19 pandemic, for example, highlighted the fragility of global supply chains, as shortages of key goods such as medical supplies and semiconductors reverberated throughout the global economy. Similarly, trade tensions between the United States and China have raised concerns about the long-term viability of relying on foreign production for critical goods.

Rome faced similar challenges as it became more reliant on its provinces for economic sustenance. As the Empire expanded, it became increasingly dependent on the flow of goods and resources from its provinces to the core. However, as political instability and military pressures grew, the provinces became less able or willing to supply the central Empire with the resources it needed. This contributed to Rome's economic decline, as the central government found it harder to fund its military, maintain infrastructure, and provide for the needs of its citizens.

In the modern West, the challenge of economic resilience in the face of globalisation and outsourcing is a pressing issue. To mitigate the risks associated with reliance on foreign production, Western nations must invest in rebuilding their domestic manufacturing capabilities, developing new technologies, and diversifying their supply chains. Failure to address these vulnerabilities could lead to a repeat of Rome's experience, where economic hollowing out and reliance on external sources of wealth contributed to the collapse of the Empire.

The Lessons from Rome Decline and the Road Ahead

The outsourcing of manufacturing in the modern West and the resulting economic challenges bear striking similarities to the economic decline of the Roman Empire. Both Rome and the modern West experienced a shift in their economic base, leading to rising inequality, social unrest, political fragmentation, and the deterioration of infrastructure. Just as Rome became increasingly reliant on its provinces for economic sustenance, modern Western economies have outsourced much of their manufacturing to lower-cost countries, creating new vulnerabilities.

The lessons from Rome's decline are clear: economic resilience and the maintenance of a strong domestic economic base are essential for the long-term stability of a civilisation. In both the Roman and modern contexts, the failure to address these challenges has had profound consequences, leading to political instability, social unrest, and ultimately, the weakening of the state. To avoid repeating Rome's mistakes, modern Western nations must invest in rebuilding their manufacturing sectors, addressing the root causes of economic inequality, and ensuring that their economies are resilient in the face of globalisation and technological disruption.

As I reflect on the economic stagnation and infrastructure collapse that contributed to Rome's decline, the parallels with the modern West are striking. Just as Rome struggled to adapt to the changing economic and political landscape, so too does the West face significant challenges. Rising inequality, inflation, crumbling infrastructure, and the disruptive forces of globalisation all point to a system under strain.

Yet, while the comparisons are sobering, history need not repeat itself in the same way. Rome's decline was a result of many factors, some of which were beyond its control. However, the modern West still can chart a different course. Addressing the economic challenges, we face will require bold and sustained action. Investment in infrastructure, both physical and digital, is essential to ensuring long-term economic growth and stability. Moreover, policies that address inequality and provide opportunities for all citizens, rather than just the wealthy few, are critical to maintaining social cohesion.

The lessons of Rome are clear: neglecting economic fundamentals and infrastructure can lead to irreversible decline. As I continue to explore in this book, the West stands at a crossroads. Whether we choose to learn from the mistakes of the past or continue down the path of stagnation and decay will ultimately determine our fate. The warnings of history are there for us to heed; the question is whether we will listen.

Chapter 4: Moral and Cultural Decline: Are We Repeating History?

The fall of the Roman Empire has long been a subject of fascination for historians, political thinkers, and civilisational theorists alike. It was not a single event, but a slow, inevitable collapse brought about by a multitude of interconnected factors economic, military, political, and cultural. Yet one element of the decline stands out more than most: the moral and cultural decay that characterised Rome in its latter years. As I reflect on our own time, I cannot help but wonder if we in the West are not merely echoing the same patterns that led to Rome's demise. Are we repeating history?

The argument that moral decay played a significant role in the fall of Rome is well-documented. Roman society, once a bastion of civic virtue, order, and discipline, slowly descended into decadence. It became a culture of indulgence, marked by a loss of civic responsibility and an erosion of the values that had once defined the empire. In parallel, the West today faces a similar crisis, one marked by the rise of identity politics, the loss of a unifying national purpose, and the breakdown of social norms. At the heart of it all lies a fundamental question: are we, like the Romans, losing our cultural cohesion, and if so, what does that mean for the future of Western civilisation?

The Moral Decay of Rome: Decadence and Fragmentation

In the twilight years of the Roman Empire, a shift occurred within its societal fabric. Once known for its disciplined citizenry and adherence to the concept of *virtus* the Roman ideal of manliness, courage, and civic duty the empire devolved into a state of decadence. Lavish banquets, excessive displays of wealth, and a general pursuit of pleasure became emblematic of the Roman elite. The famed Roman historian, Sallust, lamented this shift, writing that "ambition drove many men to become false; to have one thought locked in the breast, another ready on the tongue." This disintegration of virtue, combined with an increasing reliance on foreign mercenaries and the disengagement of Roman citizens from military service, signalled a growing internal weakness.

Civic virtue was eroded as the Roman populace became more self-serving and disengaged from the collective well-being of the state. The Roman philosopher and politician, Cicero, warned that a republic could only survive as long as its citizens were virtuous. Without that moral backbone, the political system would inevitably collapse. The loss of civic engagement, the disintegration of familial structures, and the general indulgence in pleasure rather than duty signalled a weakening society, one that was no longer capable of sustaining the complex machinery of empire.

Moreover, cultural fragmentation took root as Rome expanded. The influx of foreign peoples and cultures within its borders peoples who neither assimilated into Roman customs nor shared in its civic values exacerbated tensions. While Rome had always been a multicultural society, it had historically demanded assimilation into Roman ideals. As the empire weakened, however, this process of cultural integration broke down. The empire became a patchwork of conflicting cultures, religions, and social norms, further undermining the unity that had once held it together.

The West's Cultural Crisis: Identity Politics and Loss of Common Purpose

If we fast forward two millennia, we find ourselves in a situation eerily reminiscent of Rome's moral and cultural decline. The West, particularly in the post-Cold War era, has undergone a profound cultural transformation. Once united by a broadly shared set of values rooted in the Enlightenment principles of individual liberty, democratic governance, and the rule of law Western societies now seem fractured by the rise of identity politics and the loss of a common purpose.

The rise of identity politics, particularly in the USA, UK, and Western Europe, has fuelled a sense of division rather than cohesion. Identity politics, in its most extreme forms, encourages individuals to prioritise their group identity whether based on race, gender, or sexual orientation over their shared identity as citizens of a nation-state. While the recognition of diverse experiences is vital for any democratic society, the divisiveness of identity politics has led to an erosion of national unity. This division parallels the cultural fragmentation that plagued Rome, where the multitude of ethnic groups and foreign customs within the empire eventually led to internal discord.

Furthermore, the West today faces a crisis of purpose. In the aftermath of the Second World War, the Western world led by the United States and Europe embarked on a project of reconstruction and global leadership, aimed at promoting democracy, free markets, and human rights. This shared mission provided a sense of direction and moral clarity. But with the end of the Cold War and the rise of globalisation, that common purpose has faded. We now find ourselves in a cultural landscape where relativism reigns supreme, and where the very notions of truth, objective morality, and civic duty are called into question. Much like the Romans, who lost sight of their original mission as they grew comfortable in their decadence, we, too, risk losing our sense of collective responsibility.

The Breakdown of Social Norms and Western Moral Decay

The breakdown of social norms in Western society further mirrors Rome's decline. In Roman times, the family was once considered the bedrock of society. However, by the time of the empire's collapse, familial structures had weakened, contributing to the overall disintegration of social cohesion. Today, we are witnessing similar trends. Traditional family structures in the West have been in decline for decades, with rising rates of divorce, single-parent households, and a general devaluation of marriage and child-rearing. This breakdown of the family unit has profound consequences for societal stability, as the family is the primary institution for inculcating values, discipline, and a sense of responsibility in future generations.

The rise of hedonism and the pursuit of individual pleasure, at the expense of societal well-being, is a hallmark of late Roman decadence that resonates strongly in the modern West. This cultural shift away from collective responsibility and civic virtue toward self-gratification is evident in various facets of contemporary life, including consumerism, celebrity culture, and especially the pervasive influence of social media. As with Rome, these trends threaten to erode the moral and cultural foundations that once underpinned Western civilisation. However, when comparing the West's cultural trajectory not only with Rome but also with modern-day China, a fascinating divergence emerges.

Hedonism and Cultural Decadence: Parallels with Rome and Divergence from China

In the final centuries of the Roman Empire, the ruling elites indulged in conspicuous displays of wealth and power, detached from the everyday struggles of the broader populace. Lavish feasts, grandiose villas, and gladiatorial games symbolised a society in which personal luxury outweighed public good. The moral fabric of Roman society, which had once prized civic duty, sacrifice, and communal values, was slowly unravelled by an obsession with pleasure and status. This weakening of Rome's moral core played a significant role in its eventual collapse.

In the modern West, we see similar patterns. Consumerism has become a central aspect of life, particularly in the United States, the UK, Canada, and parts of Western Europe. The glorification of wealth and celebrity culture promotes an ideal of success defined not by contribution to the common good but by individual achievements, often based on fame or material accumulation. Social media, particularly platforms like Instagram and TikTok, have exacerbated this phenomenon, creating a virtual marketplace where status is measured in likes and followers. This relentless pursuit of digital validation mirrors the superficiality of Roman elites' public spectacles, both feeding a culture of narcissism that prioritises short-term pleasure over long-term stability.

A particularly concerning aspect of this shift is the effect it has on youth. The ubiquitous use of smartphones, particularly the iPhone, has transformed the social landscape. Face-to-face interaction is increasingly replaced by digital encounters, with significant social consequences. Studies show that excessive use of social media is linked to feelings of isolation, anxiety, and depression, as young people struggle to reconcile their real lives with the curated, often unattainable standards they see online. Just as the youth of late Rome were increasingly drawn into a world of spectacle and luxury, detached from civic values, today's youth are immersed in a digital culture that promotes self-indulgence over responsibility.

Yet, when we look at China, we see a starkly different approach to these cultural challenges. In modern-day China, the government has actively sought to curb the influence of Western-style hedonism and consumerism, especially among its youth. Regulations limiting the use of video games and social media, coupled with a strong emphasis on education and national pride, reveal a deliberate effort to steer the younger generation away from the excesses that have plagued the West. The Chinese Communist Party has long promoted a narrative of collective responsibility, economic development, and national rejuvenation values that stand in contrast to the West's focus on individual freedom and self-gratification.

While China is not without its own social and economic challenges, its leadership's ability to enforce cultural cohesion has allowed it to avoid the kind of moral and cultural fragmentation seen in the West. This difference may be attributable to China's historical emphasis on Confucian values, which prioritise hierarchy, social harmony, and duty to the collective over individual desires. In contrast, the West, much like Rome in its later years, has become increasingly individualistic, leading to social fragmentation.

The Role of Technology and Social Media in the Erosion of Civic Virtue

The modern-day obsession with social media and technology in the West has exacerbated the cultural shift toward hedonism. In many ways, social media serves the same function that the Roman arena did in its final centuries: it distracts, entertains, and isolates individuals from the larger issues facing society. Instead of engaging in meaningful discourse or fostering civic responsibility, large segments of the population especially the younger generation are absorbed in a world of selfies, memes, and viral videos. Social media algorithms are designed to maximise engagement, often by promoting content that appeals to base emotions like envy, outrage, or desire. This focus on personal gratification is reminiscent of the "bread and circuses" used by Roman emperors to pacify the populace, offering entertainment and distraction while the empire crumbled around them.

In both the West and late Rome, this shift toward personal indulgence at the expense of civic virtue undermined the foundations of society. In Rome, it was not merely the pursuit of luxury that led to decline but the moral degradation that accompanied it the loss of a sense of duty to the state and one another. Similarly, in the modern West, the focus on self-expression and personal fulfilment often comes at the cost of community engagement and collective responsibility. Youth, in particular, have become disconnected from the civic values that once underpinned Western democracies. The rise of social media platforms has created a generation that is more concerned with personal image than with contributing to the common good.

In contrast, China has taken a more authoritarian approach to managing the social impacts of technology. The government's strict control over the internet and social media platforms, combined with policies aimed at limiting screen time for youth, reflects a recognition of the dangers posed by unchecked digital influence. By controlling the narrative and curbing excesses, China seeks to maintain a sense of social harmony and prevent the kind of moral decay that has taken root in the West. This is not to say that China's approach is without flaws its restrictions on free speech and personal freedoms have raised significant ethical concerns but it does highlight the differing paths taken by East and West in response to the cultural challenges of the digital age.

Economic Structures, Taxation, and Hedonism: A Comparative Analysis of Rome, the West, and China

In addition to cultural decadence, economic structures in the West reveal troubling parallels with Rome's decline. In both cases, rising inequality, burdensome taxation, and economic stagnation eroded the middle class, leading to widespread discontent. In Rome, the wealthy elite controlled vast estates and avoided paying their fair share of taxes, while the lower classes were increasingly burdened. This unequal distribution of wealth and the failure to address systemic economic imbalances contributed to Rome's eventual collapse.

In the modern West, we see a similar situation. Tax systems in the United States, the UK, and other Western nations often favour the wealthy, with loopholes and tax havens allowing the elite to minimise their contributions. At the same time, middle- and lower-income citizens bear a disproportionate share of the tax burden. The concentration of wealth in the hands of a few has led to growing economic inequality, much like in late Rome, where the economic elite enjoyed lives of luxury while the majority of the population struggled to make ends meet. This economic disparity has been further exacerbated by globalisation and technological disruption, which have hollowed out the middle class and created a precarious economic landscape.

China, on the other hand, presents a different model. While it too faces challenges related to inequality, its centralised system of governance allows for more direct intervention in economic matters. The Chinese government has been able to implement large-scale infrastructure projects, manage its tax system more efficiently, and maintain social welfare programmes that, at least in theory, aim to redistribute wealth and promote social stability. Unlike the West, where individualism and free-market capitalism dominate, China's state-controlled economy prioritises collective goals, often at the expense of personal wealth accumulation. This approach has allowed China to avoid some of the pitfalls that have plagued the West, although it remains to be seen whether China's economic model is sustainable in the long term.

However, there is a cost to China's model. Its strict control over the economy, coupled with its limitations on personal freedom, creates an environment in which the state takes precedence over the individual, which can stifle creativity and innovation. The question remains whether China's approach will prove more resilient than the West's individualistic, market-driven model in the face of growing global economic and environmental challenges.

The Future of the West: Lessons from Rome and China

The rise of hedonism and the pursuit of individual pleasure in the modern West reflects a broader cultural and economic crisis, one that bears a striking resemblance to the conditions that led to Rome's fall. In both cases, the prioritisation of short-term gratification, whether through lavish displays of wealth or the digital indulgences of social media, has eroded the moral and civic fabric of society. This focus on personal pleasure at the expense of collective responsibility weakens social cohesion and undermines the stability of democratic institutions.

China's approach to these challenges, while not without its issues, offers a compelling counterpoint. Its emphasis on collective responsibility, social harmony, and state control stands in stark contrast to the West's individualistic ethos. However, the authoritarian nature of China's regime limits personal freedoms, raising questions about the long-term viability of its model as history has shown that socialism fails...

Ultimately, the West must decide whether it will continue down the path of moral and cultural fragmentation or whether it will take steps to revitalise the civic virtues that once underpinned its success. Like Rome, the West risks collapse if it allows economic inequality, cultural decadence, and political fragmentation to go unaddressed. However, by learning from both Rome's failures and China's successes, Western societies can chart a course toward renewal, one that balances individual freedom with collective responsibility and long-term stability.

The challenge facing the West is formidable, but it is not insurmountable. The rise of hedonism, the erosion of civic virtue, and the growing divide between rich and poor are not inevitable outcomes. They are the result of choices choices that can be changed. By addressing the cultural and economic issues at the heart of its current malaise, the West can avoid the fate of Rome and perhaps offer a path to renewal that ensures the preservation of democratic values, social cohesion, and long-term prosperity. While the parallels between the West and Rome's decline are stark, they also serve as a warning that, if heeded, could inspire a course correction.

Immigration and Cultural Fragmentation: A Crisis of Cohesion

One of the most striking parallels between the decline of Rome and the potential decline of the West today is the issue of immigration and cultural fragmentation. In the later years of the Roman Empire, large waves of migrants often from Germanic tribes flooded the empire's borders. These groups, many of whom were not assimilated into Roman culture, contributed to the weakening of the empire's internal cohesion. The failure to integrate these migrants into the Roman system of governance, values, and norms ultimately resulted in a fractured society, one that was unable to respond effectively to external threats.

In the West today, we are witnessing a similar phenomenon. The influx of immigrants, particularly from regions with cultures and values that are, in many cases, inimical to Western moral and political norms, has raised concerns about the loss of cultural cohesion. While immigration has historically been a source of strength for Western nations, the failure to adequately assimilate new arrivals into the cultural and civic framework of their host countries has led to increased social tensions. In many cases, immigrant communities remain isolated, adhering to their cultural practices and values rather than integrating into the broader society. This lack of integration exacerbates the sense of fragmentation and division, much as it did in the Roman Empire.

The issue of open borders and mass immigration is particularly relevant in the context of Europe, where the migrant crisis of recent years has posed significant challenges to social cohesion. The influx of refugees and migrants from the Middle East and Africa, many of whom come from societies with vastly different social, cultural, and religious values, has led to growing concerns about the erosion of Western identity. In some cases, these migrant communities have failed to integrate into their host societies, leading to the rise of parallel societies where Western values of democracy, secularism, and individual rights are not upheld.

Are We Repeating History?

Given the striking parallels between the moral and cultural decline of Rome and the current state of Western society, it is difficult not to conclude that we may indeed be repeating history. Like the Romans, we have become complacent in our prosperity, indulging in decadence and losing sight of the values that once defined us. Our society is increasingly fragmented, divided by identity politics, cultural relativism, and the erosion of social norms. We have lost our sense of common purpose and shared identity, and in doing so, we have weakened the very foundations of our civilisation.

Yet, unlike the Romans, we have the benefit of hindsight. We can look to history as a guide and attempt to steer our society away from the same fate that befell Rome. The question is whether we have the will to do so.

Remedies and Predictions: Avoiding Rome's Fate

The parallels between Rome's fall and the challenges faced by the modern West are clear, but there are also significant differences. For one, the Western world is far more interconnected and technologically advanced than Rome ever was. This presents both challenges and opportunities. The rapid pace of technological change has disrupted traditional economic and social structures, contributing to the sense of fragmentation and instability. Yet, it also provides us with the tools to address these challenges in ways that Rome never could.

To avoid repeating Rome's fate, we must address the root causes of our moral and cultural decline. This begins with a renewal of civic virtue and a reassertion of the values that have historically defined the West: individual liberty, democratic governance, the rule of law, and respect for human dignity. We must also work to rebuild our sense of national identity, one that is inclusive yet rooted in a shared commitment to these foundational principles.

Furthermore, we must take a more deliberate approach to immigration, one that prioritises the integration of newcomers into the cultural and civic fabric of our societies. This does not mean rejecting immigration, but rather ensuring that those who come to our shores are fully integrated into the cultural and legal norms of their host countries. Just as Rome's failure to integrate its foreign populations contributed to its decline, so too will our failure to assimilate migrants lead to further fragmentation.

Lastly, we must recognise the importance of the family as the bedrock of society. Strengthening family structures, promoting the importance of marriage and child-rearing, and fostering a sense of responsibility in future generations will be crucial to rebuilding the moral fabric of Western civilisation.

If we can address these challenges head-on, there is hope that we can avoid the fate of Rome. But if we continue down our current path one marked by moral decay, cultural fragmentation, and a loss of common purpose we may very well be doomed to repeat history.

Chapter 5: The Role of Governance: Rome's Failed Leadership vs. Modern Political Instability

As we explore the decline of great empires, one cannot overstate the pivotal role of governance in determining their fate. The collapse of the Roman Empire offers a chilling case study on how weak, short-term leadership and bureaucratic inefficiency can precipitate societal downfall. The parallels with modern Western political systems particularly in the United States, United Kingdom, Canada, and Western Europe are striking, with political instability, divided governance, and widespread public distrust in institutions eroding the fabric of our democracies.

In this chapter, I will delve into the failings of Rome's leadership and draw comparisons to the current state of political dysfunction in the West. In examining these similarities, the warning signs become increasingly clear: when governance falters, so too does the society it is meant to protect and uphold.

Rome's Weak and Ineffective Leadership

The late Roman Empire, especially after the third century AD, suffered from a chronic failure of leadership. The emperors of this period, far from the titanic figures of Rome's earlier centuries, often ruled for only a brief time before being deposed, assassinated, or replaced by someone with greater ambition but no real skill in governance. It was an era where emperors were more concerned with consolidating personal power than addressing the mounting challenges facing the empire be it external threats from barbarian tribes or internal issues of economic decay and social unrest.

One can observe a dizzying array of emperors during the third and fourth centuries, with figures such as Valerian, Gallienus, and Diocletian attempting to stave off disaster through military might and administrative reforms, but ultimately failing to prevent the empire's long-term disintegration. These rulers were caught in a vicious cycle: each emperor's brief reign was marked by attempts to fix Rome's deep-seated problems, but no one had enough time or authority to implement lasting solutions. Short-term fixes only delayed the inevitable, while the constant power struggles further drained the empire's resources.

The bureaucratic inefficiency that arose from such frequent transitions of power further compounded these problems. In a government plagued by corruption and self-interest, Rome's administrative systems became bloated and unresponsive. The overcomplication of governance, with layers upon layers of officials, tax collectors, and provincial administrators, not only alienated the populace but also failed to serve the empire's needs effectively. What was once a well-oiled machine of administration in Rome's heyday had become a sclerotic mess.

This reminds me of the current state of Western governance. In many ways, the short-termism, internal conflicts, and bureaucratic inefficiency that characterised Rome's final centuries now appear all too familiar in the political landscapes of the USA, UK, and other Western nations.

Modern Political Instability in the West

Today's political systems in the West are also marred by ineffective leadership, often driven by the same short-term thinking that contributed to Rome's decline. Election cycles, particularly in democratic countries, create an environment where politicians are incentivised to focus on immediate gains rather than long-term stability. The need to win votes encourages populist promises and superficial policies, while deeper structural issues such as wealth inequality, crumbling infrastructure, or climate change are routinely neglected or inadequately addressed.

We are witnessing a growing distrust in political institutions across Western democracies. Divided governments, exemplified by the frequent gridlock in the US Congress or the ongoing fragmentation within the European Union, hinder progress on critical issues. In the United Kingdom, the aftermath of Brexit continues to reveal the political fragility of a once-stable system. Canada, while less polarised, faces its share of challenges, including the rise of regionalism and an increasingly fractured political environment.

These divisions have not only slowed down the ability of governments to act decisively but also eroded public faith in democratic processes. Much like the Roman populace began to lose confidence in the ability of their leaders to protect and govern, so too have citizens in the West started to doubt the efficacy of their political systems. Polls across the US, UK, and much of Europe show declining trust in governmental institutions, with many feeling that their leaders are out of touch with the needs of ordinary people.

This leads to an increased appetite for non-traditional political solutions. The rise of populism across the West is one such response, echoing the political turmoil of late Rome.

The Rise of Populism and Authoritarianism

In times of political instability and ineffective governance, people often turn to strong leaders who promise to break through the deadlock and restore order. This was true in late Rome, when military strongmen such as Septimius Severus or Constantine rose to power, offering stability through force. These figures often centralised authority, marginalised traditional governing institutions, and ruled with increasing authoritarianism.

The Rise of Populism: A Response to Governance Failures

While populism is often painted in broad strokes as a destructive force, particularly by those on the left of the political spectrum, it is essential to understand that populism represents more than just a reactionary or authoritarian movement. Rather, it is the voice of a populace frustrated by systemic failures of governance, policy, and leadership that have allowed inequality, cultural disintegration, and social unrest to fester unchecked.

Populist movements across the West, represent the will of people who feel alienated by the prevailing liberal order. For decades, many in the working and middle classes have felt their concerns ignored by political elites, who, in their view, have prioritised personal gain, globalist policies, and progressive social agendas at the expense of national interests, traditional values, and economic security.

In this context, populism is not an aberration or a blip on the political radar; it is a legitimate response to a deep-rooted sense of disenfranchisement. It is a call for a return to long-held social norms and values, norms that many feel have been eroded by left-leaning, liberal leaders. The rise of populist and nationalist leaders in recent years signals a demand for policies that prioritise national sovereignty, cultural cohesion, and economic fairness over what many perceive as the excesses of globalisation, unchecked immigration, and progressive social engineering.

The argument against populism often comes from those invested in the status quo those who benefit from the political, social, and economic structures currently in place. But to simply dismiss populist leaders and their supporters as reactionary or authoritarian ignores the legitimate concerns that fuel these movements. Many ordinary citizens see populism as a necessary corrective to decades of governance that has allowed issues like mass immigration, cultural fragmentation, and economic inequality to proliferate.

Populism as a Democratic Force

It is crucial to recognise that populist movements arise within democratic frameworks and are subject to the same checks and balances as any other political force. Populism, far from being inherently authoritarian, often acts as a reassertion of democratic principles a demands that the voice of the people be heard, rather than overridden by technocrats or unelected elites. In this sense, populism can be seen as a return to the roots of democracy, where governance is more closely aligned with the will of the majority.

In countries where populist leaders have gained power, their ability to govern is still bound by democratic norms. Elections, free speech, and the rule of law remain intact, ensuring that populist leaders, like any others, are held accountable to the people. The portrayal of populist figures as inherently dangerous often stems from the discomfort of those who see their political and ideological dominance challenged. However, populist movements can serve as a valuable counterbalance to elite-driven governance, particularly when that governance strays too far from the needs and concerns of the majority.

The criticisms often levelled against populist leaders that they appeal to emotion, offer simple solutions to complex problems, or undermine established institutions are not without merit. However, these critiques fail to consider the underlying causes of populism's rise. Populism is not simply the product of demagoguery or a turn towards authoritarianism; it is a reaction to real issues that have been ignored or mishandled by mainstream political actors. Populism promises to address these concerns head-on, offering policies that resonate with the lived experiences of ordinary citizens, rather than the detached theoretical frameworks of elites.

Addressing the Root Causes of Populism

If we are to understand populism fully, we must look at the broader socio-political landscape that has given rise to it. Over the past several decades, Western democracies have faced numerous challenges, many of which have been exacerbated by the policies of left-leaning, liberal governments. These challenges include:

1. **Uncontrolled Immigration**: Many in the West feel that liberal policies on immigration have led to a dilution of cultural identity and an erosion of social cohesion. In Europe,

in particular, the influx of immigrants and refugees from the Middle East, Africa, and beyond has strained social services, heightened security concerns, and sparked debates about the compatibility of different cultural values. The public perception is that the political elite has been more concerned with promoting multiculturalism and humanitarian ideals than with safeguarding national interests and protecting the rights of native citizens.

2. **Economic Inequality**: Globalisation, while beneficial to certain sectors of society, has left others behind. Many working-class and rural populations feel abandoned by liberal economic policies that have prioritised global trade, outsourcing, and financial markets over local jobs and industries. Populism appeals to these disenfranchised groups by promising to restore economic fairness, protect jobs, and prioritise national industries over global corporate interests.

3. **Cultural Fragmentation**: The rise of identity politics, driven by progressive ideologies, has contributed to a sense of cultural fragmentation in many Western societies. Populists often reject the notion that society should be divided along lines of race, gender, or sexuality, arguing instead for a return to a unified national identity. The pushback against political correctness and progressive social norms reflects a broader desire for cultural continuity and stability.

4. **Elitism and Corruption**: A recurring theme in populist rhetoric is the idea that political elites have enriched themselves at the expense of ordinary citizens. Scandals involving corrupt politicians, corporate influence over government, and the revolving door between public office and private industry have fuelled widespread cynicism about the integrity of democratic institutions. Populism seeks to break this cycle by returning power to the people and holding

elites accountable.

By addressing these issues directly, populist movements aim to restore a sense of national pride, security, and fairness. This is not inherently authoritarian, nor is it a rejection of democratic principles. Rather, it is a demand for leadership that reflects the values and concerns of the majority. When traditional political actors fail to address these concerns, populism steps in to fill the void.

Populism as a Path to Reform

Far from being a threat to democracy, populism can serve as a force for necessary reform. It is a wake-up call to the political establishment that their policies and priorities are out of sync with the needs of their citizens. In this sense, populism can act as a corrective mechanism, ensuring that governments remain responsive and accountable to the people they serve.

While it is true that some populist leaders may employ rhetoric that challenges established institutions, this is not inherently harmful. Institutions must evolve and adapt to the changing needs of society. Populism, by challenging the status quo, can drive this evolution, pushing for reforms that strengthen democratic processes, protect national sovereignty, and promote social cohesion.

Of course, the rise of populism is not without risks. There is always the danger that populist leaders, in their pursuit of power, may undermine democratic norms or resort to authoritarian tactics. However, it is important to recognise that democracy itself provides the tools to prevent such abuses. Elections, free press, and an engaged citizenry act as safeguards against the overreach of any leader, whether populist or otherwise.

The challenge, then, is not to reject populism outright but to ensure that it remains grounded in democratic principles. By embracing the legitimate concerns of populist movements while safeguarding the core values of democracy, Western societies can navigate the current political turbulence and emerge stronger for it.

A Balanced View of Populism

In conclusion, populism must be viewed not as an inherent threat to democracy but as a reflection of the failings of current governance. It arises from genuine dissatisfaction with the liberal policies and leadership that have, in many people's view, allowed societal decay to take root. Far from being corrosive, populism offers an opportunity for democratic renewal and a chance to recalibrate governance to better reflect the will of the people.

We must remain vigilant to ensure that populist movements do not devolve into authoritarianism, but we must also recognise the value they bring in challenging the status quo and advocating for policies that resonate with a broader swathe of the population. In many ways, populism is democracy in action, a reminder that the ultimate authority in any society lies not with elites but with the people themselves.

As we continue to draw lessons from the decline of Rome, it becomes clear that governance is most effective when it aligns with the values and needs of the people. In both Rome and the modern West, the failure to address these needs has led to political instability and the rise of alternative movements.

This was certainly the case for Rome, where emperors like Diocletian and later Constantine reshaped the political landscape in ways that stifled individual freedoms and local autonomy, contributing to the empire's eventual decline. By understanding populism in this context, we can better navigate the complexities of modern governance and avoid the pitfalls that led to Rome's downfall.

We must ask ourselves if the current political climate in the West is setting the stage for a similar erosion of democratic principles. Are we, like the Romans, sacrificing long-term stability for short-term political victories?

The Cost of Political Dysfunction

Ineffective governance, populism, and authoritarianism come at a high price. In Rome, the cost was the gradual weakening of the state's ability to manage its affairs. Corruption became rampant, military overreach stretched resources thin, and the constant infighting among elites prevented any meaningful reform.

In the West today, the symptoms of political dysfunction are manifesting in similar ways. Infrastructure is deteriorating, economic inequality is widening, and social cohesion is fraying. In earlier chapters, I discussed the economic stagnation plaguing the modern West, with rising inflation, crumbling public services, and the hollowing out of the middle class. Much like in late Rome, where taxation crises and inflation ravaged the empire's economy, the West now finds itself grappling with the consequences of years of political neglect and mismanagement.

When governance fails to address these issues, societal decline accelerates. We are already seeing the rise of political polarisation, civil unrest, and even violence in some parts of the West. Public dissatisfaction with government has led to protests, riots, and in some cases, outright rebellion against the status quo.

If we fail to heed the lessons of Rome's fall, we risk heading down the same path. Weak leadership, bureaucratic inefficiency, and political instability were the hallmarks of Rome's decline, and they are becoming all too familiar in the modern West. Without a concerted effort to reform our political systems, strengthen democratic institutions, and restore public trust in governance, we may find ourselves facing a similar fate.

Remedies and Predictions

What then can be done to avoid the pitfalls that consumed the Roman Empire? I believe there are several key steps that Western societies must take if they are to prevent further decline.

First, we must prioritise long-term governance over short-term political gains. This means reforming election cycles, reducing the influence of money in politics, and encouraging policies that address systemic issues rather than temporary fixes. It also requires a commitment from political leaders to focus on the greater good rather than personal power or party interests.

Second, we must work to rebuild public trust in government. Transparency, accountability, and civic engagement are crucial here. Leaders must be held accountable for their actions, and citizens must feel that their voices are being heard. This will require structural reforms, such as greater checks and balances, as well as cultural shifts towards greater civic responsibility.

Third, the rise of populism and authoritarianism must be checked. While populist leaders may offer quick fixes, their long-term impact is often corrosive. We must defend the principles of democracy, freedom of speech, and the rule of law against those who seek to undermine them for personal or political gain.

Finally, we must look to history for guidance. The fall of Rome offers a stark reminder of what happens when governance fails. By understanding the mistakes of the past, we can better navigate the challenges of the present.

In the next chapter, I will explore another critical element of Rome's decline: moral and cultural decay. As we shall see, the loss of civic virtue and social cohesion played a key role in Rome's downfall. The question we must ask is whether Western society is now experiencing a similar crisis, and if so, how we might reverse course before it's too late.

Chapter 6: Military Overstretch: Rome's Defenses and Western Military Engagements

As I delve further into the parallels between the decline of the Roman Empire and the challenges facing the modern West, I find it imperative to address the issue of military overstretch. The vast expanse of Rome's empire and its overextended military resources bear a striking resemblance to the Western world's military engagements today. Both Rome and the West, particularly the USA and its NATO allies, have found themselves involved in long-term military commitments, often at the cost of their internal stability and external dominance. In this chapter, I will explore how the Roman Empire's military overreach contributed to its downfall and draw comparisons with the contemporary Western world's military entanglements, particularly in conflicts like those involving Russia and Ukraine, the Iranian proxies, the threat of China over Taiwan, and the precarious position of Israel.

Rome's Overextended Borders: A Cautionary Tale

At its height, the Roman Empire stretched from Britain in the north to Egypt in the south, from the Iberian Peninsula in the west to the far reaches of Mesopotamia in the east. Such vast territorial expansion came with significant military challenges. Rome's legions, once the most disciplined and formidable fighting force in the ancient world, found themselves scattered across immense frontiers, tasked with defending territories far from the empire's core. The famous Rhine and Danube rivers served as natural boundaries, but the constant threat of invasion from so-called "barbarian" tribes Visigoths, Ostrogoths, Vandals, and Huns made defence a perpetual concern.

The strain on Rome's military was exacerbated by its increasing reliance on mercenaries, often recruited from the very barbarian tribes they sought to keep at bay. While this strategy may have seemed pragmatic at first, it ultimately weakened the cohesiveness of Rome's military apparatus. These mercenaries had little loyalty to the Roman state, and their motivation was financial rather than patriotic or ideological. When Rome could no longer afford to pay these foreign soldiers, many of them turned against the empire, accelerating its decline.

The fall of Rome's western half in 476 AD was precipitated by the sack of the city by the Visigoths in 410 AD and later by the Vandals in 455 AD. These invasions demonstrated the fatal consequences of an overstretched and under-resourced military. The Roman army, once feared by all, could no longer defend its capital, let alone the far-flung provinces that had come to depend on its protection.

NATO and Western Military Commitments: Echoes of Rome

In the modern West, we see a similar pattern of military overstretch. The United States, along with its NATO allies, has been involved in numerous long-term military engagements since the end of the Second World War. From the Korean War to the Vietnam War, from the invasion of Iraq to the ongoing conflict in Afghanistan, Western powers have consistently committed vast resources to military interventions across the globe. These conflicts have often been justified in the name of maintaining global stability, promoting democracy, or containing hostile powers. However, much like Rome, the Western military machine has found itself stretched thin, both financially and strategically.

Take, for instance, the ongoing war between Russia and Ukraine. While NATO has not been directly involved in the fighting, the West has provided Ukraine with extensive military and financial aid. This assistance has not only drained resources but has also heightened tensions with Russia, a nuclear-armed power. The conflict, which has no clear end in sight, risks dragging the West into a prolonged proxy war with one of its most formidable adversaries. The parallels to Rome's overextended borders are stark. Just as Rome was unable to defend its entire frontier, the West today faces the challenge of defending its interests in multiple theatres of conflict simultaneously.

The withdrawal of U.S. forces from Afghanistan in 2021 was a moment that will likely go down in history as emblematic of weak leadership, not just in terms of strategy but also in political foresight and international perception. This episode, in which a great military power hastily exited from a region it had occupied for two decades, bears striking similarities to Rome's retreat from its far-flung provinces in the waning days of the empire. In both cases, feckless and indecisive leadership led to a loss of credibility, both at home and abroad, while exposing underlying weaknesses that had been festering for years.

The Unilateral Withdrawal: A Symbol of Decline

The way the United States, under the Biden-Harris administration, executed the withdrawal from Afghanistan serves as a potent reminder of the consequences of military overreach and political short-sightedness. For two decades, the U.S. and its NATO allies had invested trillions of dollars in Afghanistan, attempting to build a stable government and military that could withstand the insurgency of the Taliban. Yet, the decision to abruptly withdraw, without a coherent exit strategy or adequate planning for the aftermath, led to the immediate collapse of the Afghan government and military. The scenes of chaos at Kabul airport, with desperate Afghans clinging to departing planes, will be remembered as a stark symbol of Western failure.

From a geopolitical standpoint, the decision to pull out unilaterally, without proper coordination with NATO allies, not only left Afghanistan in disarray but also sent a message of weakness to adversaries around the world. China, Russia, and Iran all countries with vested interests in the region quickly capitalised on the perception that the U.S. was no longer a reliable global leader. The Taliban's swift return to power was not just a failure of military policy but a failure of Western diplomacy and leadership.

In comparison to Rome, we see similar missteps in how the empire managed its distant provinces. By the 5th century AD, the Roman Empire had stretched itself too thin, unable to effectively govern or defend its far-flung territories. The empire's withdrawal from Britain in 410 AD is a case in point. Facing pressures on multiple fronts from Germanic tribes in the east, the Visigoths in Italy, and internal instability Rome's leadership decided to pull its legions out of Britain, leaving the island vulnerable to invasions by the Saxons, Angles, and Jutes. The sudden and hasty withdrawal left the local population unprotected and marked the beginning of what would be centuries of instability and fragmentation in Britain.

Just as Rome's retreat from Britain signalled the empire's waning influence, the U.S. withdrawal from Afghanistan signals a similar decline in Western authority. In both cases, a once-powerful state, overstretched and unable to maintain its military commitments, chose to abandon a territory it had invested in, leaving behind chaos and a power vacuum.

Feckless Leadership: Rome and the U.S.

Weak and ineffective leadership is a recurring theme in the decline of empires, and the U.S. withdrawal from Afghanistan fits squarely into this pattern. In Rome's case, the final centuries of the Western Empire were marked by short-term rulers, political infighting, and a lack of cohesive vision. From the 3rd century onwards, the empire experienced what is known as the "Crisis of the Third Century," a period during which dozens of emperors rose to power only to be swiftly deposed or assassinated. The lack of strong leadership during this time weakened Rome's ability to respond to external threats and manage internal divisions, leaving the empire vulnerable to barbarian invasions.

The U.S. withdrawal from Afghanistan was not merely the failure of a single administration, but the culmination of two decades of inconsistent and often contradictory policies. Successive American presidents, Bush, Obama, Trump, and Biden struggled to define a clear objective for the U.S. mission in Afghanistan. Was it nation-building? Counterterrorism? Establishing democracy? The lack of a coherent and unified strategy, coupled with shifting political priorities, led to a prolonged engagement with no clear end in sight.

Biden's decision to withdraw, though politically popular at home, was executed in a manner that demonstrated a lack of foresight and strategic planning. The U.S. had failed to build a stable Afghan government capable of standing on its own, much like Rome's failure to develop loyal provincial governments that could manage territories in the absence of Roman legions. In Afghanistan, the collapse of the Afghan military and government mirrored Rome's abandonment of its provincial clients, who, without the backing of Roman legions, quickly fell to external invaders.

In both cases, leadership chose short-term solutions to long-term problems. For Rome, it was the decision to withdraw from provinces like Britain, North Africa, and parts of Gaul, in the face of rising costs and diminishing resources. For the U.S., it was the decision to prioritise political expediency and domestic pressure over the long-term consequences of leaving a fragile region vulnerable to hostile forces.

Loss of Credibility and Geopolitical Ramifications

The U.S. withdrawal from Afghanistan damaged its credibility on the global stage, much like Rome's gradual retreat from its borders eroded the confidence of its allies and subjects. After Rome's withdrawal from Britain, the local population felt abandoned, while the empire's neighbours and enemies interpreted the retreat as a sign of weakness. Similarly, America's allies, particularly in NATO, were left scrambling to respond to the consequences of the hasty U.S. departure. Countries like the UK and Germany, which had also committed forces to Afghanistan, were blindsided by the decision and left dealing with the humanitarian fallout.

Russia and China took note of the U.S. withdrawal. For Russia, it reinforced the belief that the U.S. was a declining power, no longer willing or able to sustain its global military commitments. This perception likely emboldened Vladimir Putin's decision to escalate his war in Ukraine. Just as the barbarian invasions of Rome accelerated after the empire's withdrawal from its frontiers, hostile powers like Russia and Iran now see opportunities to expand their influence in the absence of decisive Western leadership.

China, too, sees the withdrawal as an opportunity to assert itself more forcefully in its sphere of influence, particularly in Taiwan. The U.S. has long been committed to defending Taiwan from Chinese aggression, but the withdrawal from Afghanistan raises questions about America's willingness to stand by its allies in a prolonged conflict. Much as Rome's inability to defend its territories in the west emboldened tribes to raid and invade, the U.S.'s perceived retreat from global commitments could embolden China to take more aggressive action in the Pacific.

The Costs of Overextension: Rome and the U.S.

Underlying both the Roman and American withdrawals is the issue of military and economic overextension. Rome, by the 5th century, could no longer afford to maintain the vast military presence required to defend its borders. The empire had stretched itself too thin, and its financial resources were being drained by the constant need to fortify its frontiers, pay mercenaries, and respond to internal rebellions. Similarly, the U.S. has been engaged in perpetual warfare for the past two decades, with wars in Iraq and Afghanistan costing trillions of dollars and exacting a heavy toll on the military and the national budget.

The decision to withdraw from Afghanistan was, in part, driven by the recognition that the U.S. could no longer afford to sustain an indefinite military presence in the country. Much like Rome's decision to withdraw from Britain, the U.S. was forced to cut its losses and retreat. However, the cost of overextension is not just financial; it is also reputational. Rome's retreat from its provinces sent a message to its enemies that the empire was in decline. Likewise, the U.S. withdrawal from Afghanistan signals to adversaries like China and Russia that America may no longer be willing to invest in its global military commitments.

Feckless Leadership, Then and Now

As I reflect on the parallels between Rome and the U.S., the withdrawal from Afghanistan stands as a potent symbol of weak leadership and military overstretch. In both cases, decisions driven by short-term political pressures led to long-term consequences that weakened the state's ability to project power and maintain stability. Rome's retreat from its borders, coupled with weak and divided leadership, hastened its fall. Similarly, the U.S. withdrawal from Afghanistan, executed with little foresight or planning, may well be remembered as a turning point in the West's global decline.

To avoid Rome's fate, the West must learn from its mistakes. Strong, decisive leadership is crucial, as is a clear and coherent strategy that prioritises long-term stability over short-term political gains. The West must also recognise the limits of its military power and avoid the temptation to overextend itself in conflicts that offer little strategic value. If it fails to heed these lessons, the withdrawal from Afghanistan may prove to be just the beginning of a much larger unravelling. The spectre of Rome's fall looms large, and history, if left unheeded, may well repeat itself.

In addition to the war in Ukraine, the threat posed by China's ambitions over Taiwan represents another potential flashpoint. The USA, bound by its commitment to Taiwan's defence, could find itself embroiled in a conflict with China, a rising global superpower with formidable military capabilities. The West's focus on maintaining a global military presence in the South China Sea, the Middle East, Eastern Europe, and beyond echoes Rome's decision to spread its legions across vast and disparate territories, leaving itself vulnerable to threats both foreign and domestic.

Mercenaries, Contractors, and the Modern Military Complex

Another parallel between Rome and the West is the increasing reliance on mercenaries or, in today's terms, private military contractors. The use of contractors in conflicts like Iraq and Afghanistan has become a hallmark of modern Western military operations. These contractors, while highly trained and efficient, are often motivated by profit rather than loyalty to any state. This mirrors the mercenary forces that Rome relied upon in its later years, which similarly lacked a deep-rooted connection to the Roman state and its ideals.

When the Roman Empire could no longer pay its mercenaries, they turned against it, hastening its downfall. While Western nations today still maintain the ability to pay their private contractors, the reliance on these forces raises questions about the long-term sustainability of such an approach. As Western military budgets come under increasing strain, particularly in the face of rising domestic needs, one wonders whether the modern West might suffer the same fate as Rome, with its hired guns becoming a liability rather than an asset.

Learning from Rome: The Perils of Overextension

The lessons from Rome's military overstretch are clear: no empire, no matter how powerful, can sustain an indefinite military presence across the globe without risking internal collapse. For the modern West, the temptation to maintain global dominance through military interventions must be tempered with a sober assessment of the costs involved. The wars in Iraq and Afghanistan alone have cost trillions of dollars, resources that could have been better spent on domestic infrastructure, education, and healthcare. Instead, much like Rome, the West has prioritised military dominance over internal stability.

The current global landscape, with the rise of China, Russian aggression, and the proliferation of non-state actors like ISIS and Hezbollah, presents a formidable set of challenges to Western military strategy. This dynamic, however, is not without historical precedent. In the later stages of the Roman Empire, the rise of external threats from the Germanic tribes to the Huns and Vandals forced Rome to focus on military solutions to secure its borders, while the internal weaknesses of the empire, from economic fragility to political corruption, went largely unaddressed. This failure to recognise and tackle the root causes of instability hastened Rome's decline, and the parallels with the West today are striking.

The Rise of China and the Resurgence of Russian Aggression

China's emergence as a global power has reshaped international relations, much in the way that the rise of powerful barbarian groups like the Goths and Huns shifted the balance of power on Rome's frontiers. For decades, the United States and its Western allies enjoyed unchallenged military and economic dominance, much as Rome did during its zenith. However, just as Rome underestimated the capacity of foreign powers to evolve and challenge its authority, the West may have been slow to respond to China's strategic rise.

China's Belt and Road Initiative, aggressive territorial claims in the South China Sea, and military modernisation efforts are signs that it is not content to remain a regional power but aspires to global influence. This mirrors how the Huns and Visigoths, once confined to the periphery of Roman lands, gradually built up their strength and became significant players in the empire's eventual undoing.

Russia, similarly, has become increasingly emboldened under Vladimir Putin, with its actions in Crimea and Ukraine recalling the constant threats Rome faced from neighbouring powers. Rome's inability to respond effectively to repeated incursions by hostile forces on its borders weakened the empire militarily and undermined its standing in the eyes of both allies and enemies. The West's inconsistent response to Russia's aggressive actions has had similar effects, with Western nations divided over the appropriate level of response, just as Rome's internal divisions hampered its ability to act decisively.

The invasion of Ukraine by Russia in 2022 echoed the sort of opportunistic aggression that Rome faced in its final centuries. As Rome struggled to maintain control over its far-flung territories, local rulers and external enemies took advantage of moments of perceived weakness. Russia, recognising the West's hesitancy to fully confront it militarily, may have been similarly emboldened. This is exacerbated by the energy dependence many Western European countries have on Russia, much like the economic entanglements Rome found itself in with hostile groups that had come to rely on the empire's resources.

The Proliferation of Non-State Actors

The rise of non-state actors like ISIS and Hezbollah adds another layer of complexity to Western military strategy. These groups, with their ability to operate outside traditional state frameworks, are akin to the roving bands of mercenaries and tribal groups that frequently disrupted Roman territory. While Rome often sought to hire these groups as federates or mercenaries, trusting them to act in the empire's interest, they often turned against Rome or operated with divided loyalties. In modern times, the West has similarly engaged with various local militias, rebel factions, and proxies in conflict zones like Syria, Iraq, and Afghanistan, often with mixed results.

Hezbollah, for instance, operates with considerable autonomy while receiving support from Iran, positioning itself both as a political actor and a militant force in Lebanon. Its operations against Israel, often through proxy warfare, resemble the proxy conflicts that plagued Rome, with various groups exploiting Rome's internal weaknesses for their gain. The proliferation of groups like ISIS, which defy conventional military engagement due to their fluid and decentralized nature, is a modern equivalent of the guerrilla tactics employed by barbarian groups that overwhelmed Roman defences.

These non-state actors have proven difficult to counter with traditional military force, much as Rome's reliance on its legions proved ineffective against the hit-and-run tactics of the invading Goths and Vandals. The West's inability to fully eliminate these groups, despite substantial military spending, reflects a fundamental strategic miscalculation rooted in a failure to address the socio-political conditions that give rise to such groups in the first place.

Iran's Influence and the Biden Administration's Strategy

Iran's role in modern geopolitical conflicts is another significant challenge for the West. The Biden administration's diplomatic overtures towards Iran, particularly concerning the 2015 nuclear deal (Joint Comprehensive Plan of Action, JCPOA), have been seen by critics as an appeasement strategy. While the administration has sought to limit Iran's nuclear ambitions through diplomacy, the consequences of this approach have been heavily debated. Detractors argue that easing sanctions has allowed Iran to continue supporting militant groups like Hezbollah, Hamas, and the Houthis, emboldening them to act against Western interests and its allies, particularly Israel.

Rome, too, faced a similar dilemma when dealing with hostile external powers. In the later years of the empire, Rome often sought peace treaties with barbarian groups like the Visigoths and Ostrogoths, paying them in gold or land to prevent further invasions. These appeasement strategies provided temporary relief but did little to solve the broader issues of declining military power and internal instability. Much like Iran today, these groups took advantage of Rome's internal weaknesses and used their newfound resources to expand their influence at the empire's expense.

The Biden administration's approach to Iran mirrors Rome's attempts to buy time through diplomacy, rather than addressing the root causes of instability in the Middle East namely, corruption, sectarian conflict, and the disenfranchisement of populations that fuel support for groups like Hezbollah and ISIS. By lifting some sanctions on Iran, the U.S. has allowed Tehran to increase its funding of proxy groups across the region, particularly those targeting Israel. This is reminiscent of how Rome, by making concessions to barbarian groups, only delayed the inevitable conflict.

The Overreliance on Military Spending

In response to these growing threats, Western nations have increasingly turned to military spending as a solution, rather than addressing the underlying causes of conflict. The U.S. defence budget remains the largest in the world, and NATO countries have been pressured to increase their military spending in response to Russian aggression and China's rise. However, much like Rome's heavy investment in its military during the later years of the empire, this focus on military solutions comes at the expense of addressing deeper socio-political and economic issues.

Rome's later strategy of fortifying its borders and hiring more mercenaries ultimately failed because it did not address the internal decay that was weakening the empire from within. The Western empire, beset by economic troubles, corruption, and political instability, could no longer effectively project its power, no matter how many soldiers it hired or how many walls it built. The same dynamic is at play today in the West. By focusing on military spending to counter external threats, Western governments are neglecting the root causes of instability poverty, inequality, political disenfranchisement, and corruption in conflict-prone regions.

In the Middle East, for example, the West's military interventions have failed to bring about long-term stability. The invasion of Iraq in 2003, the intervention in Libya in 2011, and the ongoing conflicts in Syria and Yemen have all been driven by military objectives, yet none have produced a lasting peace. These interventions have, in many cases, exacerbated the very conditions that give rise to groups like ISIS and Hezbollah, much like Rome's military campaigns against barbarian tribes often ended in temporary victories but long-term instability.

Western reliance on military might to solve complex geopolitical issues, without addressing the underlying socio-political dynamics, risks repeating the mistakes of Rome. Just as Rome's military victories over groups like the Goths and Vandals were short-lived, the West's military successes in places like Iraq and Afghanistan have not led to sustainable peace or security. The failure to invest in nation-building, governance reform, and economic development in these regions has left them vulnerable to the very forces the West sought to defeat.

Lessons from Rome's Decline

The lesson from Rome's fall is clear: military power alone cannot sustain an empire. Rome, at its height, was the most formidable military force in the world, but its failure to address internal decay economic inequality, political corruption, and social fragmentation made it vulnerable to external threats. The West today faces a similar challenge. While it remains militarily powerful, its internal divisions, economic inequalities, and political instability threaten to undermine its ability to respond effectively to the challenges posed by China, Russia, and non-state actors like ISIS and Hezbollah.

Western nations must learn from Rome's mistakes and adopt a more holistic approach to global security. Military spending is necessary, but it cannot be the only solution. Addressing the root causes of conflict poverty, corruption, political disenfranchisement, and social inequality will be critical to ensuring long-term stability. Just as Rome's reliance on fortifications and mercenaries failed to prevent its collapse, the West's focus on military solutions, without addressing deeper socio-political issues, risks leading it down a similar path.

In conclusion, the rise of China, Russian aggression, and the proliferation of non-state actors present significant challenges to the West, but they are not insurmountable. However, if Western nations continue to rely solely on military spending and appeasement strategies, without addressing the root causes of instability, they risk repeating the mistakes of Rome. The West's strength lies not only in its military power but in its ability to build stable, inclusive societies. If it fails to do so, the decline of the Roman Empire may serve as a stark warning of what lies ahead.

Conclusion: Avoiding the Fate of Rome

As I reflect on the parallels between Rome's military overstretch and the modern West's military engagements, it becomes clear that history offers a stark warning. Rome's downfall was not solely the result of external pressures; it was the culmination of internal decay exacerbated by overextension abroad. The modern West, with its vast military commitments and reliance on private contractors, risks repeating Rome's mistakes.

The Decline of Civic Virtue and Social Cohesion

One of the most significant consequences of Rome's military overextension was the decline of civic virtue and social cohesion. As the empire became increasingly militarized, the Roman populace became disengaged from the civic life that had once defined Roman identity. The concept of *civitas*, or active participation in public affairs, was gradually replaced by a focus on personal gain and the accumulation of wealth. This decline in civic virtue contributed to the fragmentation of Roman society, making it more vulnerable to external threats.

In the modern West, there is a similar decline in civic engagement and social cohesion. Political apathy is on the rise, particularly among younger generations, who feel disillusioned with a political system that seems more interested in maintaining global dominance than addressing the pressing concerns of ordinary citizens. The rise of populism, both on the right and the left, can be seen as a response to this disengagement, as people seek alternatives to the political status quo. However, much like the rise of authoritarian rulers in late Roman history, these movements often exacerbate division rather than fostering unity.

The West's overreliance on military might and its neglect of social cohesion is reminiscent of Rome's failure to invest in its internal stability. By focusing on external threats, Western governments risk losing the trust of their citizens, much as Rome lost the loyalty of its provinces. The social contract between the governed and the governors is at risk of breaking down, as citizens grow increasingly frustrated with leaders who prioritise military engagements over domestic needs.

Strategic Withdrawal: A Necessary Shift

To avoid the fate of Rome, the West must learn to prioritise. Rather than seeking to maintain a global military presence at all costs, it would be wise to focus on securing key strategic interests while investing in the long-term stability of its societies. This does not mean a complete withdrawal from the global stage, but rather a more measured approach to military engagements. The U.S. and its allies should focus on strengthening alliances, such as NATO, and securing critical regions, like the Indo-Pacific, where China's rise presents a significant challenge to Western interests.

Strategic withdrawal does not equate to defeat but rather a realignment of priorities. Rome, at various points in its history, attempted to consolidate its forces by abandoning territories that were no longer worth defending. Emperor Hadrian, for example, famously built Hadrian's Wall to define the empire's limits in Britain, acknowledging that certain areas could not be held without overextending Roman resources. A similar approach could benefit the West today. Rather than trying to maintain a military presence in every conflict zone, the West should focus on defending key interests while supporting the development of local governance and stability in conflict-prone regions.

This would require a shift in thinking, moving away from a purely military-based approach to foreign policy and towards a more holistic strategy that addresses the root causes of conflict such as poverty, corruption, and political disenfranchisement. Military force can only provide temporary solutions to these issues, and without a broader focus on economic development, governance reform, and social cohesion, the conditions that give rise to instability will persist.

Conclusion: Heeding Rome's Warning

The fall of the Roman Empire serves as a powerful reminder of the limits of military power. Rome's failure to address its internal decay while overextending its military resources ultimately led to its downfall. The modern West faces a similar set of challenges, with rising external threats from powers like China and Russia, and the proliferation of non-state actors like ISIS and Hezbollah. However, the greatest threat to Western stability may come not from these external forces, but from within.

If Western leaders do not learn to prioritise and focus on securing key strategic interests while addressing the internal decay of their societies, they may find themselves on the brink of collapse, overburdened by the weight of military commitments they can no longer sustain. The West must heed the lessons of Rome, or risk repeating its fate.

This chapter ties into the themes explored earlier in this book, particularly in Chapter 5, where I examined the role of governance in Rome's decline and the political instability facing the West today. Weak leadership and internal divisions contributed to Rome's inability to effectively manage its military resources, just as divided governments in the West struggled to formulate coherent military and foreign policies. Moreover, the moral and cultural decline discussed in Chapter 4 is intertwined with the issue of military overstretch, as societies that lose their sense of purpose and cohesion often turn to militarism as a means of asserting their power on the world stage.

In the chapters that follow, I will explore further how the West might avoid the fate of Rome. But for now, military overstretch, if not addressed, will be a critical factor in determining the future of Western civilisation. The warning signs are there whether the West will heed them remains to be seen.

Chapter 7: Immigration and Integration: From Barbarian Tribes to Modern Migrants

The migration of people, whether driven by war, economic necessity, or the lure of opportunity, has always been a powerful force in shaping the course of civilisations. As I explore the parallels between the fall of the Roman Empire and the potential decline of the modern West, one of the most glaring similarities is the role of mass migration and the challenges of integration. The Roman Empire, like the West today, was confronted by an influx of people from beyond its borders. For Rome, it was the so-called barbarian tribes; for the West, it is the waves of migrants from various regions, particularly the Middle East, Africa, and parts of Asia. Both periods are marked by the failure to properly integrate these new arrivals, which led to severe strains on social cohesion, governance, and security.

The Role of Mass Migration in the Decline of Rome

The late Roman Empire faced tremendous challenges in managing the waves of migrants that entered its territories. The Visigoths, Ostrogoths, Vandals, and other barbarian tribes, initially seeking refuge from the advancing Huns or driven by their expansionist desires, were not simply invaders they were also refugees and settlers. Rome's borders were vast, and in many cases, it allowed these groups to settle within its provinces. The intent was often to assimilate them into Roman culture, perhaps even to bolster Rome's declining manpower and economy. However, as I have explored in earlier chapters, Rome was already struggling with political instability, economic stagnation, and military overextension. The administrative apparatus necessary to integrate these peoples was severely weakened, and as a result, these new arrivals often remained outside the fabric of Roman society.

One of the most famous examples of this failure to integrate was the settlement of the Visigoths. In 376 AD, they were allowed to cross the Danube River and settle within the Empire, ostensibly as allies. However, mistreatment and exploitation by Roman officials led to resentment, culminating in the Battle of Adrianople in 378 AD, where the Roman army suffered a catastrophic defeat at the hands of the Visigoths. This event marked the beginning of the end of Roman control over its territories in the West. The failure to integrate these newcomers, combined with the inability to manage internal conflicts and external threats, gradually eroded the Empire's strength.

The comparison between the migration challenges faced by the Roman Empire and those confronting the modern West is indeed striking. Both periods witnessed large-scale migration driven by external factors whether the movements of the Visigoths, Vandals, and other Germanic tribes into Roman territories or the waves of migrants fleeing conflicts in the Middle East, economic hardship in Africa, and instability elsewhere today. In both cases, the challenge is not only the sheer number of migrants but also the deep cultural, religious, and societal differences they bring with them, making integration a fraught and difficult process.

In Rome's case, the arrival of the Visigoths and other barbarian groups marked a significant turning point in its decline. By the fourth and fifth centuries, the Roman Empire was already under immense pressure, facing internal political instability, economic decay, and military overstretch. The Visigoths, initially fleeing the Huns and seeking refuge within Roman borders, were allowed to settle in Roman lands, but the Empire struggled to manage their integration. Far from being absorbed into the Roman social fabric, the Visigoths maintained their distinct cultural identity and operated as a separate force within the Empire. This resulted in friction, culminating in the sack of Rome by the Visigoths under Alaric in 410 AD a symbolic moment that underscored Rome's vulnerability and its inability to control the groups it had allowed within its borders.

In modern times, Western nations are experiencing similar pressures. The influx of migrants into Europe, particularly since the Syrian civil war and the broader instability in the Middle East and North Africa, has tested the capacity of Western governments to manage migration flows. Much like the Visigoths, many of these migrants are fleeing war, persecution, and economic collapse. While Western nations, particularly in Europe, initially responded with humanitarian efforts offering asylum and support there has been a growing realisation that these large-scale migrations present profound challenges to the social fabric of these countries.

Cultural and Religious Differences: A Barrier to Integration

One of the most pressing issues for both Rome and the modern West is the cultural and religious differences that complicate integration. In the Roman Empire, the Visigoths, Vandals, and other tribes came from vastly different backgrounds compared to the Roman population. Many of these groups adhered to Arian Christianity, a variant of Christianity considered heretical by mainstream Roman Catholicism at the time. This religious difference created tension within the Empire, not only in terms of faith but also in political and social cohesion.

These groups were not merely culturally distinct but were also politically autonomous in many ways, with their tribal leaders and systems of governance. Rome's inability to fully assimilate them into its societal framework meant that they remained separate and often hostile entities within the Empire's borders. The gradual settlement of these tribes transformed the Roman landscape, as they carved out territories of their own, leading to the fragmentation of Roman authority and contributing to the Empire's eventual downfall.

In modern Western nations, the situation bears striking similarities. Migrants arriving from the Middle East, Africa, and South Asia often come from countries with radically different cultural and religious traditions. Many of these migrants, particularly from Muslim-majority countries, hold views that are in stark contrast to the liberal democratic values of the West particularly in areas such as gender equality, secularism, and individual rights. The challenge of integrating such diverse populations is immense, and in many cases, the process has been marked by the formation of isolated, insular communities within Western cities.

This is not to suggest that all migrants resist integration or that all Western countries have failed in their integration policies. However, the reality is that a significant number of migrants, especially those arriving in large numbers over a short period, have struggled to assimilate into the cultural norms of their host nations. This has led to the emergence of "parallel societies," where immigrant communities maintain their distinct cultural practices, often at odds with the values of the broader society. In cities across Europe from Paris to London to Berlin, there are now neighbourhoods where integration has largely failed, and where the rule of law is challenged by religious or ethnic customs that differ from those of the host country.

The resulting tension is not unlike that seen in late Rome, where the Visigoths, Vandals, and other barbarian groups operated as semi-independent entities within Roman territory. These tribes often maintained their own military forces, governance structures, and customs, undermining the central authority of the Roman state. The parallels to modern-day Europe are clear: many Western countries now face the dilemma of how to maintain social cohesion in the face of large, culturally distinct immigrant populations that resist full integration.

The Consequences of Failed Integration

The Roman Empire's inability to integrate these barbarian tribes led to a series of cascading crises that further weakened its political and military structure. The Visigoths, once allowed into Roman territory, soon became a destabilising force. The Empire's failure to provide them with the resources and protections they had been promised led to unrest, culminating in the Battle of Adrianople in 378 AD, where the Roman army suffered a devastating defeat at the hands of the Visigoths. This battle is often seen as a turning point in Rome's decline, as it demonstrated the Empire's vulnerability to internal threats. Over time, other groups followed the Visigoths' example, exploiting Rome's weakened state and further fragmenting the Empire.

Similarly, in the modern West, the failure to integrate large migrant populations poses a long-term threat to social cohesion and political stability. In countries such as France, Germany, and Sweden, there have been growing concerns about the rise of radicalisation within immigrant communities, particularly among second and third-generation migrants who feel alienated from the broader society. The wave of Islamist terrorist attacks across Europe in recent years is perhaps the most visible manifestation of this failure to integrate, but the broader social consequences are just as significant.

Tensions between immigrant communities and the native population have led to the rise of right-wing populist movements across Europe and North America, as native citizens increasingly feel that their governments are failing to protect their cultural heritage and national identity. This is reminiscent of the rise of internal divisions in Rome, where different regions of the Empire began to assert their independence from central authority. As I explored in Chapter 5, these internal divisions were one of the key reasons for Rome's decline, and the modern West risks following a similar trajectory if it cannot resolve the tensions created by large-scale immigration.

In the United States, the situation is slightly different but no less concerning. While the US has a long history of immigration, recent years have seen an increase in illegal immigration from Central and South America, leading to significant political polarization. Much like the debates over immigration in Europe, the issue has become a lightning rod for broader societal divisions. Some argue that immigration strengthens the nation by bringing in new talent and perspectives, while others see it as a threat to social cohesion and national security. The inability to reach a consensus on how to manage immigration whether through more robust border controls or better integration policies mirrors Rome's inability to handle the influx of barbarian tribes effectively.

Rome's Elites and the Failure to Act

A key factor in Rome's failure to manage migration was the role of its elites, who were often more concerned with their wealth and power than with the long-term health of the Empire. The Roman aristocracy, insulated from the immediate effects of barbarian settlement, viewed these migrations through the lens of short-term economic gain. Barbarian tribes provided a cheap source of labour and mercenaries, which the elites used to shore up their estates and bolster their private armies. This short-sightedness, however, contributed to the gradual erosion of Roman power. By the time the elites realised the full extent of the threat posed by the barbarian presence within their borders, it was too late.

In the modern West, we see a similar dynamic at play. Many political and economic elites have promoted mass immigration as a means of addressing labour shortages or boosting economic growth. In some cases, particularly in industries such as agriculture, construction, and low-wage service sectors, the influx of migrants has been seen as a boon for business. However, this short-term economic benefit often comes at the cost of social cohesion. As we have seen with the rise of populist movements across Europe and the US, many native citizens feel that their governments are prioritising the interests of big business and political elites over the well-being of the broader society.

Moreover, like Rome, today's elites are often disconnected from the everyday realities of mass migration. While working-class communities bear the brunt of the social and economic pressures created by large-scale immigration, the elites are largely insulated from these effects. This disconnect has only fuelled resentment among the native population, much as it did in Rome, where the common citizens increasingly felt abandoned by their leaders.

The failure of Western governments to address these concerns risks deepening the divisions within society and accelerating the process of decline. Just as Rome's elites ultimately found themselves unable to control the forces they had unleashed, modern Western elites may soon find that their policies of mass immigration and cultural relativism have created a situation beyond their control.

Can the West Learn from Rome's Mistakes?

The lessons from Rome's failure to manage migration are clear: successful integration requires more than just allowing migrants to enter; it requires a concerted effort to assimilate them into the cultural, political, and social fabric of the host nation. Rome's failure to do so led to its eventual collapse, as the barbarian tribes it had allowed within its borders gradually took over large portions of the Empire.

For the modern West, the challenge is similar. To avoid the fate of Rome, Western nations must find a way to integrate migrants while maintaining the core values and cultural identity that define their societies. This means enforcing the rule of law, promoting shared democratic values, and ensuring that migrants are given the tools and opportunities to contribute meaningfully to their new societies.

However, this also requires a recognition that not all cultural practices are compatible with the principles of liberal democracy. While diversity can be a strength, it must be balanced with a commitment to the values that have made the West successful. Just as Rome struggled to maintain its identity in the face of mass migration, the modern West must confront the difficult question of how to preserve its cultural heritage while welcoming newcomers. If it fails to do so, it risks repeating the mistakes of history, with potentially catastrophic consequences.

Modern Immigration Challenges: Integration, Social Cohesion, and Cultural Conflicts

In the United States, the United Kingdom, Canada, and across Western Europe, immigration has become one of the most divisive political issues. At its core, the debate is about integration. Can Western societies effectively integrate these new populations while maintaining social cohesion? Or, as in the case of Rome, will the inability to integrate lead to fragmentation and decline?

One of the most visible signs of strain is the rise of populist movements in response to mass immigration. As I explored in Chapter 5, these movements are often characterised by a sense of cultural and economic displacement among native populations, who feel that their governments have failed to protect their interests. Much like the Roman populace who watched as barbarian tribes settled within their borders, modern Western citizens are concerned about the long-term impact of mass migration on their way of life.

Integration is not just a matter of economics or social services; it is also a question of cultural identity. In many Western countries, the incoming migrants come from cultures that are, at times, radically different from the secular, liberal democracies they enter. The West has long prided itself on values such as individual freedom, gender equality, and secular governance. However, many of the migrants arriving in recent decades come from more conservative, religiously oriented societies, leading to inevitable clashes over issues such as women's rights, freedom of speech, and religious expression. In some cases, the failure to address these differences has led to the development of parallel societies, where migrant communities live in isolation from the broader national culture.

This is not unlike the situation Rome faced in its later years. The Empire was increasingly divided between those who still adhered to traditional Roman values and the new arrivals who maintained their own distinct identities. Over time, these divisions contributed to the weakening of the Empire's cohesion. Similarly, in the West today, the failure to integrate large immigrant populations risks creating a fractured society, where different groups live alongside one another but do not truly share a common identity.

Can Lessons from Rome's Handling of Migration Provide Insights for Modern Western Nations?

One of the most critical lessons from Rome's experience is the importance of having a clear and coherent policy for integrating migrants. Rome, particularly in its later years, often reacted to migration in an ad hoc manner, allowing large groups of people to settle without fully considering how they would be incorporated into the Empire's political, social, and economic systems. The result was a patchwork of communities that were often at odds with one another and with the Roman state itself.

The challenge of modern Western nations in dealing with migration is a critical issue, one that shares profound similarities with the Roman Empire's experiences with the so-called barbarian tribes during its decline. When I suggest that successful integration requires more than simply providing economic opportunities, I am reflecting on the necessity of a broader cultural and social integration something the West today is struggling with, much as Rome did in its later years.

In the modern context, migration is not solely a matter of legal or controlled immigration but also of widespread illegal migration, a phenomenon that has profound socio-political and economic ramifications. Illegal migration, particularly in Western Europe and the United States, has become a matter of grave concern, creating tension within these societies over the question of identity, cultural assimilation, and social cohesion. Like Rome, the West is grappling with a crisis of identity, where cultural relativism and the breakdown of shared norms are weakening the societal glue that once held these nations together.

The West's Crisis of Identity and the Struggle with Integration

Cultural relativism, which emphasises that all cultural practices are equally valid, has complicated the West's ability to enforce a cohesive set of values. This is evident in the debate over how to integrate migrant populations who may come from vastly different socio-political and religious backgrounds. The challenge is that while modern liberal democracies pride themselves on tolerance and diversity, this sometimes leads to a reluctance to impose the cultural norms that have historically underpinned their society's norms such as individual liberty, gender equality, and the rule of law.

As I discussed in earlier chapters, this is eerily like Rome's failure to enforce its cultural norms on the barbarian groups that entered its territories. Rome's elites, particularly during the late Empire, had become increasingly disconnected from the traditional Roman values that had built the Empire in its heyday. There was a growing emphasis on luxury, personal wealth, and political power, while the idea of a shared Roman identity began to fade. Barbarian tribes, once considered outsiders, were increasingly allowed to maintain their cultural practices, even as they settled deeper within Roman lands. This ultimately led to a fragmented society, where large swaths of the population no longer felt a strong allegiance to Rome itself.

Similarly, in the modern West, identity politics has led to a fragmentation of what was once a more unified cultural identity. Political correctness and the fear of offending cultural sensitivities have at times prevented Western nations from effectively integrating migrants. Instead of promoting a balanced approach that respects cultural differences while insisting on a shared commitment to democratic values, there has been a tendency to allow the formation of isolated communities where integration is minimal.

Who Profits from Illegal Migration?

Illegal migration, especially in the West, has become an industry, with many actors profiting from the chaos. This includes human traffickers who exploit vulnerable populations, political entities that seek to gain influence from the chaos of unmanaged borders, and even certain corporate interests that benefit from a cheap, often exploitable workforce. In the United States, for instance, there has been criticism that some industries, such as agriculture, construction, and hospitality, rely heavily on undocumented workers, who can be paid lower wages and who lack the legal protections afforded to citizens or legal residents.

This exploitation mirrors what occurred in late Roman society, where certain elites profited from the inflow of barbarian labour and soldiers. The Roman aristocracy, increasingly disconnected from the common Roman citizenry, grew rich off the spoils of the Empire's vast territories, including the incorporation of barbarian groups. Many of these elites welcomed the influx of barbarians as they provided cheap labour or could be conscripted into the military. However, this short-term economic gain came at a long-term cost: the erosion of Roman identity and loyalty. The elites, focused on their wealth and power, did not prioritise the social and cultural integration of these groups, much as today's political and business elites often neglect the long-term implications of allowing large numbers of unassimilated migrants into Western societies.

Current administrations, both in Europe and the United States, often face accusations of being complicit in this exploitation. Policies that fail to address the root causes of illegal migration, or that even tacitly encourage it, can be seen as serving the interests of powerful groups that benefit from cheap labour, political patronage, or the undermining of national cohesion for ideological purposes. This is reminiscent of how Rome's later emperors and senators failed to address the growing disunity within the Empire, as their focus remained on consolidating personal power rather than on preserving the integrity of the state.

Comparison to Rome's Elites and the Current Administrations

The Roman elites, especially during the final centuries of the Western Roman Empire, became increasingly detached from the well-being of the broader populace. Their wealth insulated them from many of the immediate dangers that plagued the average Roman citizen, such as the rising costs of living, barbarian incursions, and the deterioration of public infrastructure. Instead, these elites often viewed the incoming barbarian tribes as a resource to be exploited. They sought to control this migration for their benefit, using barbarian soldiers as mercenaries to fight their wars or employing barbarian labour in their vast estates.

A similar phenomenon is visible in the modern West. Today's political and economic elites are often insulated from the direct impacts of illegal migration. While working-class communities in the West bear the brunt of the economic competition, social tension, and strain on public services caused by large-scale immigration, the elites benefit from the economic advantages it brings cheap labour, a broader consumer base, and in some cases, a politically malleable population. The rhetoric of inclusivity and diversity is often used to justify mass migration, but the reality on the ground is that integration is poorly managed, leading to the formation of isolated communities that do not fully assimilate into the host culture.

In Rome's case, this failure to integrate resulted in increasing divisions within the Empire. Barbarian groups left to their own devices maintained their distinct identities and were often more loyal to their tribal leaders than to Rome. Eventually, these groups would carve out their kingdoms within the Empire, contributing to its ultimate collapse. Modern Western nations risk a similar fate if they fail to properly integrate migrant populations and allow parallel societies to develop.

Today's elites, like those of Rome, may be profiting in the short term from the current situation, but they are sowing the seeds of long-term instability. As these migrant populations grow and become more politically influential, there is the potential for significant social and political upheaval. The Roman Empire was not conquered by a single catastrophic event but rather by a gradual erosion of its internal coherence. The barbarians did not so much conquer Rome as they were invited in and gradually took over a weakened system. Similarly, the West risks weakening itself from within, as illegal migration and poor integration policies erode the social cohesion that is essential for a stable society.

A Balanced Approach to Migration and Integration

The solution lies in finding a balance between preserving the cultural identity of the West and ensuring that migrants are properly integrated into society. This does not mean a wholesale rejection of migration Rome, at its height, was a cosmopolitan empire that thrived on its diversity. However, it maintained a strong Roman identity, which newcomers were expected to adopt. The modern West must do the same. Rather than allowing identity politics to fragment society further, Western nations need to promote the values that have made them successful in democracy, individual rights, and the rule of law while encouraging migrants to adopt these principles.

Rome's failure to do so led to its eventual downfall. As I have explored in previous chapters, the decline of Rome was a gradual process, marked by economic stagnation, military overextension, and political instability. The failure to integrate migrant populations was not the only cause of Rome's fall, but it was a significant factor in the weakening of the Empire's internal cohesion. Modern Western nations would do well to heed this warning.

If the West continues down its current path failing to integrate large migrant populations, allowing illegal migration to flourish, and prioritising short-term economic gain over long-term social stability it risks repeating the mistakes of Rome. The lessons of history are clear: a strong, cohesive society cannot survive without a shared identity and a commitment to its founding principles. The West must rediscover this sense of purpose if it hopes to avoid the fate that befell the Roman Empire.

Furthermore, Rome's reliance on barbarian groups to supplement its military forces provides a cautionary tale for today's Western powers. As I discussed in Chapter 6, Rome's military overstretch and dependence on foreign mercenaries eventually contributed to its downfall. Today, Western nations are increasingly reliant on immigrant labour in sectors ranging from healthcare to construction, and even within the military itself. While this can provide short-term benefits, it also carries risks if these individuals do not feel a sense of loyalty or belonging to their host countries.

In this sense, the modern West must find a way to integrate migrants not just economically, but socially and politically, ensuring that they are fully invested in the future of their new homes. Failing to do so could lead to the same kind of internal divisions that plagued Rome in its final centuries.

Conclusion: The Warning of History

The story of Rome's decline offers a stark warning for the West today. Mass migration, if not managed carefully, can strain a society's resources, undermine social cohesion, and contribute to political instability. Rome's inability to integrate the barbarian tribes that entered its territories was a key factor in its eventual collapse. The West must learn from this lesson if it hopes to avoid a similar fate.

As I have explored throughout this book, the parallels between the Roman Empire and the modern West are numerous and troubling. In this chapter, I have highlighted the dangers of failing to integrate new populations and the consequences this can have for social cohesion and political stability. However, the West is not destined to follow Rome's path. With careful planning, a commitment to shared values, and a clear vision for the future, it is possible to navigate the challenges of mass migration and build a more cohesive, resilient society.

In the end, the question is not whether migration will continue it undoubtedly will but whether the West can rise to the challenge of integration. History suggests that the stakes could not be higher.

Chapter 8: Economic and Political Corruption: A Tale of Two Empires

Corruption, inefficiency, and the abuse of power are as old as civilisation itself. It is no surprise that these vices were part and parcel of the decline of Rome, and they find their echoes in the modern Western world. As I delve deeper into this parallel, the comparison between Rome's late-stage corruption and the political and economic challenges of the West today becomes ever more striking. In this chapter, I seek to explore how corruption served to hollow out the Roman Empire from within, and how the same forces are at work undermining the modern institutions upon which Western nations have built their success.

We are all too familiar with the image of the later Roman Empire a bureaucratic machine riddled with inefficiency, where the buying and selling of offices became a common practice. Rome's civil service, once a model of competence and efficacy, devolved into a bloated apparatus. The abuse of power became commonplace, and the very idea of public service was sacrificed for personal gain. The comparison with the modern West, especially the United States and Europe, is hard to miss. The corruption we see today whether in the form of corporate lobbying, financial irresponsibility, or the revolving door between politics and industry mirrors the deterioration that occurred in Rome.

In late Rome, the desire to attain power and influence came at a price, quite literally. Wealthy individuals could purchase prestigious offices, not to serve the Empire, but to enrich themselves. This trend undermined both the stability of the administration and the public's trust in its institutions. Those who held power were often more interested in self-preservation and personal enrichment than in addressing the real challenges facing the Empire, such as fiscal mismanagement, internal security, and the defence of its borders. This lack of accountability paved the way for the collapse of governance.

In today's Western world, we see a similar pattern. While we may not have literal buying of offices in most cases, the effect of corporate influence and lobbying is disturbingly similar. Politicians, especially in the US, are often beholden to powerful interest groups, which shape policy decisions for their benefit. Whether it's fossil fuel industries dictating environmental regulations or tech giants influencing data privacy laws, the lines between public good and private interest have blurred dangerously. I see this as a corrosive force within our democracies, where the will of the people is increasingly overshadowed by the power of money.

The financial irresponsibility of Rome in its later years was another clear marker of its decline. The Empire found itself in a constant state of financial crisis, driven by costly military campaigns, crumbling infrastructure, and the increasing demands of maintaining control over vast territories. To address these issues, the government resorted to rampant taxation and debasement of currency, which only served to exacerbate the problems. Inflation soared, trade routes became less secure, and the wealth gap between the ruling class and the common citizen widened to unsustainable levels.

Today, we face a remarkably similar set of challenges. Western nations, particularly the US, the UK, and parts of Europe grapple with soaring national debts, rising inflation, and growing economic inequality. Politicians from across the political spectrum offer short-term solutions often in the form of massive borrowing or monetary manipulation without addressing the underlying issues. Public services, much like Rome's overtaxed provinces, are crumbling under the weight of fiscal irresponsibility. The parallels are as stark as they are unsettling.

One must also consider the impact of corruption on the moral fabric of both societies. For Rome, the endless cycle of graft and mismanagement undermined the very idea of civic duty. The state, once a symbol of shared Roman values and identity, became little more than a tool for personal advancement. This moral decay was one of the key contributors to the weakening of the Empire's internal cohesion, making it easier for external forces, such as barbarian tribes, to capitalise on its vulnerability.

In the West today, there is an undeniable erosion of faith in democratic institutions, much as there was in the Roman Empire during its decline. This disillusionment with governance has become a central theme in the politics of the 21st century. As citizens perceive their governments to be either corrupt or ineffectual, it has fuelled widespread discontent. This discontent manifests in various ways, most prominently through the rise of populist movements that seek to challenge the existing order. The question then arises: are these movements a democratic correction to corruption and inefficiency, or do they risk plunging us into authoritarianism if the underlying issues are not addressed?

To understand this, it is essential to compare the current state of Western democracies to the disintegration of political integrity in Rome. The Roman Empire, especially in its later stages, became infamous for its corruption and for fostering an environment where personal gain far outweighed public duty. Just as Roman emperors and officials abused their positions for wealth and status, modern politicians are often perceived as beholden to corporate interests and the wealthy elite, rather than to the citizens they were elected to serve. This perception is a powerful driver of disillusionment and political instability today.

Populism and Discontent: Rome's "Bread and Circuses" vs. Modern Democracy

Populist movements in the US, UK, and Europe have emerged as responses to this erosion of faith in the system. Citizens, frustrated by what they see as self-serving elites, have turned to leaders who promise to restore power to the people. These movements, however, often carry the risk of authoritarian tendencies, just as Rome's responses to internal unrest frequently resulted in strongman rule. The Roman elite, in an attempt to placate a discontented populace, turned to the infamous "bread and circuses" strategy providing food and entertainment to distract citizens from the real issues of governance.

In the modern West, while bread and circuses may take different forms, the principle is eerily similar. Today, we see governments and elites offering distractions through consumerism, media, and superficial political promises. In the US, for example, populist leaders like Donald Trump capitalised on the deep-seated frustration with a perceived political establishment, promising to "drain the swamp." Meanwhile, Brexit in the UK was fuelled by a disillusionment with an elite seen as out of touch with ordinary citizens. Both movements highlight the degree to which corruption and political dysfunction have undermined trust in traditional governance.

Yet, as in Rome, these populist corrections may offer only temporary relief. Rome's bread and circuses provided short-term stability but failed to address the systemic issues plaguing the Empire. In the West today, populist leaders often promise drastic solutions to corruption and inefficiency but may lack the capacity or genuine will to implement meaningful reform. As a result, citizens may once again find themselves disillusioned, realising that the leaders they turned to in frustration are unable to fulfil their promises. This cycle risks deepening political instability and even paving the way for more authoritarian forms of government.

The European Perspective on Corruption

In 2024, European citizens remain deeply sceptical about their government's efforts to address corruption. Reports indicate that 65% of Europeans believe that high-level corruption cases are not sufficiently pursued, and only 30% think that government efforts to combat corruption are effective. Even more telling, 68% of citizens consider corruption to be widespread in their Member States. These statistics suggest a profound crisis of trust in governance, with citizens increasingly viewing their political systems as compromised and unable to serve the public good.

The UK's response to corruption has been fraught with challenges. Scandals involving parliamentary expenses, lobbying, and preferential treatment for corporations have only served to deepen public mistrust. The perception that politicians in Westminster are more interested in lining their own pockets than in serving the country has become a persistent theme in British politics. The Brexit movement, in many ways, was a manifestation of this discontent, with many voters feeling that the political establishment had abandoned them in favour of globalised elites.

In the US, the situation is equally dire. The influence of corporate lobbying, the revolving door between business and politics, and the overwhelming influence of money in elections have led many to believe that democracy is being subverted by special interests. This disillusionment has fuelled not only the rise of populist figures but also widespread cynicism about the ability of the political system to address pressing issues such as income inequality, healthcare, and corruption itself.

Canada, while often seen as more stable, is not immune to these pressures. The country has seen its corruption scandals, such as the SNC-Lavalin affair, where Prime Minister Justin Trudeau faced accusations of political interference in a legal case involving a powerful corporation. Such incidents have contributed to a growing sense of disillusionment among Canadians, who, like their counterparts in Europe and the US, are becoming increasingly sceptical of their political institutions.

Rome's Bread and Circuses: A Failed Response to Decline

The comparison to Rome is striking when we consider how political elites in the modern West attempt to placate a dissatisfied populace. In the late Roman Empire, the emperors used the provision of free grain and large-scale entertainments gladiatorial games, chariot races, and other public spectacles to distract the people from the mounting crises of the state. These spectacles were designed to provide a sense of stability and normalcy, even as the Empire's economic, military, and political foundations were crumbling.

While there is no modern equivalent of the Colosseum, the distractions offered to citizens today are no less effective. Consumerism, social media, and the constant barrage of entertainment and news can serve as modern-day circuses, keeping people engaged and distracted while systemic problems fester. In the US, the culture of constant consumption and the spectacle of political theatre often overshadow deeper issues like income inequality, healthcare access, and political corruption. The focus on celebrity politics, media soundbites, and superficial debates mirrors Rome's focus on bread and circuses, as it diverts attention from the critical failures within the system.

In the European Union, efforts to placate public dissatisfaction often come in the form of symbolic measures rather than substantive reforms. Politicians might announce anti-corruption drives, but as the statistics show, few Europeans believe these efforts are genuine or effective. This growing cynicism mirrors the attitudes of Roman citizens in the later Empire, who had little faith in the ability of their rulers to address the Empire's real problems. As a result, many turned inward, becoming more interested in personal survival than in the health of the state, a development that hastened the Empire's collapse.

Corruption and the Threat to Democratic Institutions

The erosion of faith in democratic institutions poses an existential threat to the stability of Western nations. Just as in Rome, where corruption and inefficiency undermined the legitimacy of the state, modern Western democracies are at risk of losing the trust of their citizens. In the US, for instance, the belief that the system is rigged has led to growing support for populist and anti-establishment candidates. But if these candidates fail to address the underlying issues of corruption and inequality, the cycle of disillusionment will continue, leading to further instability.

In Rome, the inability to address corruption led to a weakening of the central government's control, with local elites and provincial governors increasingly acting in their self-interest. The centralisation of power became an illusion, as the Empire's bureaucracy became so riddled with inefficiency that the state could no longer effectively govern its territories. This decentralisation of authority contributed to the fragmentation of the Empire and its eventual collapse.

In Western democracies today, the danger lies not so much in decentralisation but in the polarisation and fragmentation of political life. As citizens lose faith in democratic institutions, they become more susceptible to authoritarian solutions. We have already seen this in the rise of strongman leaders in both Europe and the US, who promise to cut through the inefficiency and corruption of the existing system. While these leaders may claim to offer solutions, their methods often undermine democratic norms and further weaken the institutions that are supposed to safeguard the public interest.

Lessons from Rome for the West

The comparison to Rome provides a sobering lesson for the modern West. Corruption, if left unchecked, erodes not just the efficiency of governance but the very fabric of society. In Rome, corruption and the resulting inefficiency contributed to the Empire's inability to respond effectively to external threats, from barbarian invasions to economic collapse. In the West today, the inability to tackle corruption and political dysfunction similarly undermines the capacity of governments to address the challenges of our time, whether they be economic inequality, immigration, or military overstretch.

The rise of populist movements in the West is emblematic of a deeper malaise within modern democratic societies. It reflects a growing discontent among citizens who feel that their voices are no longer being heard by a political class that appears detached from the daily struggles of ordinary people. While populism is often dismissed as a dangerous reactionary force, it is crucial to understand that its foundations lie in legitimate grievances. Much like the citizen revolts and unrest that Rome experienced in its later years, modern populism is not simply a product of demagoguery but rather an expression of a desire for better governance and the restoration of perceived lost values.

The West today, especially the US, UK, and many parts of Western Europe, finds itself in a precarious position. Populist movements have surged in response to the perceived failures of left-wing, liberal governments that have embraced what some would see as a progressive, quasi-socialist agenda. The parallels to Rome are striking, as, during the Roman Empire's decline, citizens often looked for strong leaders who promised to restore stability, justice, and traditional Roman values. These leaders, while initially seen as reformers, often became despots themselves, undermining the very institutions they were meant to protect. This risk is also present today, where populist leaders can easily veer into authoritarianism if the systems they inherit are fundamentally broken or if the social contract is already too frayed.

The Rise of Populism as a Democratic Correction

Populism in its essence is a cry for reform and a call to re-establish the bond between the people and their government. When viewed from this perspective, populism is not inherently destructive but is, in fact, a natural corrective mechanism within a democratic system. It is a plea for a return to competent governance, an insistence on safety, the rule of law, and the preservation of a society's social and cultural identity. In Rome, this took the form of citizens rallying around charismatic generals and provincial leaders who promised to restore order amidst the chaos of a crumbling state.

Today, however, populism is often portrayed in a negative light, particularly by left-leaning governments and the media. This perception is not entirely without basis, given that populist movements can, under the right conditions, morph into something far more dangerous. But at its core, modern populism represents a demand for good government one that ensures low crime, economic opportunity, and the protection of a society's values and identity. These are not radical demands; they are the very foundation of a functional democracy.

The political left, with its embrace of more globalist, multicultural, and socialist policies, has often been perceived as having abrogated these fundamental responsibilities. The rapid push for progressive policies without consideration of their impact on traditional communities has alienated a significant portion of the electorate. This alienation has created the perfect breeding ground for populism. The desire for safety, stability, and cultural continuity has been dismissed by some left-wing governments as regressive or intolerant, further deepening the divide. The comparison to Rome is apt here: just as the later Roman emperors became increasingly disconnected from the realities of provincial life, today's Western elites are often seen as living in a bubble, insulated from the real-world impact of their policies.

Populism and the Left's Failure: Parallels with Rome

The rise of populism can, in many ways, be traced back to the failures of the political left in recent decades. In the US, for instance, the Democratic Party's shift towards socialism, identity politics, mass immigration and other progressive causes has been met with resistance by many traditional voters who feel that their concerns over economic opportunity, safety, and cultural values are being ignored. This is particularly pronounced in rural and working-class communities, which have become disillusioned by the left's focus on what they see as elite concerns. The result has been a profound shift in political allegiance, with many former Democrats turning to populist figures like Donald Trump, who offered them the promise of a return to "traditional American values."

The situation in Europe is similar. In countries like France, Italy, and the UK, left-wing governments have been accused of prioritising progressive social policies over the needs of the working class. The French Yellow Vest movement, the Brexit vote in the UK, and the rise of far-right parties in the UK, Italy, Poland and Hungary are all manifestations of this discontent. These movements are often dismissed by the political left as reactionary or xenophobic, but to do so is to misunderstand their underlying causes. At their core, these are movements driven by people who feel that their governments have abandoned the basic tenets of good governance: safety, economic stability, and cultural continuity.

This was precisely the situation in the late Roman Empire. As the central government became more focused on maintaining its power and less concerned with the well-being of its citizens, local leaders and strongmen began to emerge as alternatives. These figures, like the populist leaders of today, promised a return to stability and security. But as history shows, these promises often led to the concentration of power in fewer hands and the erosion of democratic norms. Julius Caesar's rise, for example, was driven by a populist agenda that promised to address the grievances of the lower classes. Yet his ascent marked the beginning of the end for the Roman Republic, as it ultimately paved the way for the autocratic rule of the emperors.

The "Orwellian" Nature of Modern Governance: Left-Wing Authoritarianism?

The notion that modern left-wing governments have strayed into Orwellian territory is not without merit. George Orwell's *1984* warned of a society where truth is malleable, where the state dictates what is to be believed, and where dissent is crushed. In many ways, the current political climate bears eerie similarities to this dystopian vision. The rise of cancel culture, the suppression of dissenting viewpoints, and the increasing tendency of governments to monitor and control the flow of information have created an atmosphere of fear and conformity.

This is particularly pronounced in the US and parts of Europe, where governments and media often seem to act in concert to promote certain narratives while silencing others.

The left's use of progressive ideals as a cover for authoritarian tendencies can be seen in its approach to social issues. The imposition of speech codes, the stigmatisation of opposing viewpoints, and the demonisation of traditional values have created a society where people are afraid to speak their minds. In Rome, a similar dynamic emerged as the emperors sought to consolidate their power. Under rulers like Diocletian and Constantine, the Roman state became increasingly autocratic, using a combination of propaganda, coercion, and state-sponsored religion to maintain control over a fractured society. While the modern West has not reached this level of control, the parallels are concerning.

Bread and Circuses Redux: Modern Distractions and the Decline of Civic Engagement

The Roman strategy of "bread and circuses" was not merely a means of placating the masses; it was a deliberate attempt to distract citizens from the Empire's failings. By providing free grain and spectacular entertainment, the emperors sought to create the illusion of stability and prosperity, even as the Empire was crumbling from within. Today, the West has its versions of bread and circuses. The relentless focus on entertainment, consumerism, and digital distractions serves a similar purpose. People are so engrossed in their screens and social media feeds that they often overlook the slow erosion of their rights and the decay of their societies.

In the US, for instance, the constant churn of political theatre and media spectacles keeps citizens distracted from more serious issues like economic inequality and political corruption. The obsession with celebrity politics and the endless cycle of scandals and outrage has turned politics into a form of entertainment rather than a forum for meaningful debate. This focus on superficiality over substance mirrors

Rome's late-stage decadence, where the citizens, having lost faith in their leaders, turned to the Colosseum for diversion while the Empire rotted from within.

The same pattern is evident in Europe, where politicians often resort to symbolic gestures and empty promises rather than tackling the root causes of societal discontent. This focus on appearances over action is a hallmark of declining empires. As the Roman historian Tacitus famously wrote, "They create a desert and call it peace." In the modern context, we could say, "They create a distraction and call it governance."

Populism as a Warning, Not a Solution

The lesson from Rome is clear: populism is a symptom, not a cure. It arises when governments fail to fulfil their most basic responsibilities to their citizens. The Roman Empire's descent into autocracy began with the rise of populist leaders who promised to restore the Republic, only to undermine it further. Today, the West risks repeating this mistake. If populist movements are not met with genuine reform, they will become more radical, leading either to the rise of authoritarian leaders or to social fragmentation and collapse.

The way forward lies in recognising the legitimate grievances that fuel populism and addressing them through meaningful change. This means restoring the rule of law, ensuring that governments are accountable to their citizens, and respecting the social and cultural values that form the bedrock of democratic societies. If the West can learn from Rome's mistakes, it may yet avoid the fate of the Empire. If not, we may be witnessing the final act in the long decline of Western civilisation a decline not caused by external enemies, but by the internal corruption and disintegration of the very values that once made it great.

The lesson from Rome is clear: reform must be genuine, systemic, and aimed at restoring public trust. Otherwise, the seeds of discontent that have been sown will grow into something far more dangerous, threatening the stability and integrity of the West, much as they did for Rome.

In the end, the fate of the West is not sealed. While the comparison to Rome offers warnings, it also offers hope. Rome may have fallen, but its lessons endure. If Western democracies can learn from the past and address the corruption and inefficiency that threaten them today, there is still time to avert the fate that befell the Roman Empire. However, the window for reform is narrowing, and the future will depend on whether we can heed the empire's warning.

But what are the lessons to be drawn from Rome's experience with corruption, and can they provide any guidance for the West today? For Rome, the inability to rein in its corrupt officials led to the collapse of its administrative capacities. The provinces, which had once provided the lifeblood of the Empire, became sources of rebellion and economic drain. The lessons for the modern West are clear: without serious reform, the West's political and economic systems are at risk of becoming similarly unsustainable.

Efforts to curb corruption and restore accountability are paramount if we are to avoid a similar fate. In my earlier chapter, *The Role of Governance: Rome's Failed Leadership vs. Modern Political Instability*, I touched upon the failures of leadership in both Rome and the West. The issue of corruption, however, cannot be resolved solely through leadership changes. It requires a systemic overhaul stricter regulations on lobbying, transparent governance practices, and, perhaps most importantly, a renewed sense of civic responsibility. Without these, the slow slide into decline becomes almost inevitable.

The increasing concentration of wealth and power in the hands of a few also mirrors Rome's fate. In the Empire's later years, wealth inequality reached staggering levels, with the elite consolidating vast tracts of land and wealth at the expense of the broader population. This concentration of power led to the disenfranchisement of the Roman middle class, and eventually, to the collapse of the economic order upon which the Empire had been built.

Today, we see a similar concentration of wealth in Western societies. The wealthiest individuals and corporations wield an extraordinary amount of influence, and the gap between the rich and the poor continues to widen. This growing inequality threatens the social fabric of our societies, much as it did in Rome. When large segments of the population feel that they have no stake in the system, it breeds resentment and instability. I explored this issue in detail in my chapter on *Economic Stagnation and the Collapse of Infrastructure*, where I drew comparisons between Rome's failing economic systems and the precarious state of modern Western economies.

To avoid the fate of Rome, Western nations must address these growing inequalities. This means implementing policies that promote economic fairness, whether through tax reform, increased public investment, or initiatives aimed at improving social mobility. Failure to do so will likely lead to the same kind of social unrest and economic stagnation that plagued Rome in its later years.

Moreover, the abuse of power by political and economic elites can only be curbed if there is a cultural shift towards greater accountability. In Rome, the notion of *virtus* the Roman idea of civic virtue and duty declined significantly in its later years. The state became less about the collective good and more about personal enrichment. In much the same way, I see a decline in the idea of public service in the West today. The emphasis on personal gain, coupled with a disregard for the well-being of the wider population, is a troubling parallel.

The consequences of unchecked corruption, both economic and political, are clear: it accelerates decline, erodes trust in institutions, and leads to a society's fragmentation. I have traced these themes throughout the earlier chapters of this book whether it be in Rome's overstretched military, its ineffective governance, or its economic collapse. Corruption touches every part of a society, and once it has taken hold, it is difficult to reverse. It was the rot at the heart of Rome, and it threatens to be the same for the West today.

In conclusion, the lessons from Rome's downfall are clear. Corruption, if left unchecked, corrodes the very foundations of a society. The modern West must take heed of this warning, for the parallels are too stark to ignore. Whether it's the influence of corporate money in politics, the growing concentration of wealth and power, or the erosion of public trust in democratic institutions, the West is facing many of the same challenges that led to Rome's collapse. Only through serious reform, both political and economic, can we hope to avoid a similar fate. As I explore further in subsequent chapters, particularly in the discussion on military overstretch and the role of governance, the challenges are many but so too are the opportunities for renewal. The future is not set in stone, and the lessons of history, if heeded, can still offer us a way forward.

Chapter 9: The Collapse of Public Faith: Religion, Civic Duty, and Decline

The fall of the Roman Empire offers us numerous lessons about the fragility of even the most powerful civilisations. Among the many causes of its eventual decline, the collapse of public faith in religion, civic duty, and societal institutions stands out as a significant contributing factor. Much like the Roman Empire, the modern West faces a similar crisis today, though the forms may have evolved. The erosion of public trust in government, media, and the broader societal fabric is creating fissures in our ability to maintain a cohesive society. In this chapter, I explore these historical parallels and how the weakening of civic duty, combined with religious fragmentation and growing individualism, threatens the very foundations of Western stability.

Religious Fragmentation in Rome and the West

In the later stages of the Roman Empire, religion underwent a series of shifts that not only destabilised the societal structure but also fragmented the once-unified sense of public duty. Initially, Rome's polytheistic religious practices were a source of cohesion, giving citizens and elites alike a shared sense of purpose, divine protection, and societal order. However, as Christianity gained prominence, it increasingly split Roman society. Rather than enhancing civic unity, the adoption of Christianity as the state religion in the 4th century led to conflicts between the new Christian orthodoxy and the traditional Roman pagan beliefs, dividing the populace along religious lines.

The rise of Christianity also marked a shift away from the civic religiosity that had bound Romans together in support of their empire. The Christian focus on the afterlife often led to a retreat from worldly concerns, diminishing the importance of public service and collective responsibility that had previously characterised Roman civic duty. As Gibbon noted in *The Decline and Fall of the Roman Empire*, this religious transformation weakened the military and governmental institutions by fostering passivity, as Christian doctrine in its early years often emphasised spiritual devotion over civic engagement.

In modern Western society, we are witnessing a similar fragmentation, albeit in a more secular form. The West, once largely united under a Christian moral and cultural framework, is now deeply divided along religious and ideological lines. While religious adherence is declining, secular ideologies and identity politics have filled the void, often pitting various groups against one another. The moral cohesion once provided by shared religious and cultural values is fading, and with it, the sense of civic duty and common purpose is weakening.

The increasing secularisation of Western societies, particularly in Europe, has had profound implications for public life. In countries such as the UK and France, church attendance has plummeted, and the once-dominant Christian moral framework has become marginalised. The United States, while still more religious than its European counterparts, is also experiencing a steady decline in religious affiliation, particularly among younger generations. As religious institutions lose influence, the secular ideologies that have replaced them often promote individualism over collective responsibility, mirroring the fragmentation seen in late Roman society. The question remains: can a society maintain cohesion and stability without a unifying belief system or shared set of values?

The Erosion of Civic Duty

Closely tied to the fragmentation of religious and ideological beliefs is the erosion of civic duty. In the Roman Empire, public service and participation in civic life were once considered sacred duties. Roman citizens took pride in their contributions to the state, whether through military service, public office, or other forms of civic engagement. However, as the empire grew more corrupt and its leadership more detached from the common people, the sense of civic responsibility eroded. Citizens began to see the state not as a shared project but as an oppressive force and public trust in institutions collapsed.

This erosion of civic duty was further exacerbated by economic inequality and the rise of a professional military that was increasingly disconnected from the citizenry. In earlier times, Roman soldiers were also citizens, often landowners, who had a vested interest in defending their homeland. By the time of the late empire, however, the military had become largely composed of foreign mercenaries, and the connection between military service and civic responsibility had been severed.

In modern Western society, we see a similar decline in civic engagement and public trust. Voter participation rates are dropping in many democracies, and public confidence in government institutions is at an all-time low. In the United States, for instance, trust in Congress hovers around historic lows, and in the UK, political scandals and inept governance have led to widespread disillusionment. The decline in civic duty is not limited to political participation; it extends to all aspects of public life, from volunteering and community involvement to basic adherence to laws and societal norms.

One of the most alarming trends is the growing perception that the state no longer works for the common good but serves the interests of a privileged few. This perception, rooted in the financial crises of the 21st century and exacerbated by political corruption, mirrors the attitudes of late Roman citizens who felt increasingly alienated from their rulers. Just as Romans grew disillusioned with an empire that seemed to favour elites over the common people, so too are modern Western citizens growing sceptical of governments perceived to be under the influence of corporations, lobbyists, and financial elites.

Declining Public Trust in Institutions

In late Roman times, the loss of trust in governmental institutions was a key factor in the empire's collapse. Corruption, inefficiency, and political infighting rendered the central authority ineffective. The

Roman bureaucracy, once the envy of the world, became bloated, inefficient, and corrupt. Public offices were bought and sold, and officials often enriched themselves at the expense of the empire. As a result, the populace grew increasingly distrustful of their leaders and unwilling to support the state in times of crisis.

The situation today in the West is disturbingly similar. Public trust in institutions has been eroded by years of political scandals, economic inequality, and government failures. From the 2008 financial crisis to the COVID-19 pandemic, Western governments have repeatedly failed to live up to the expectations of their citizens. In the United States, trust in the media, government, and even the electoral process has been undermined by partisan polarisation, misinformation, and corporate influence. In the UK, the Brexit referendum exposed deep divisions within the population and shook public confidence in the political class. Across Europe, rising populism and disillusionment with the European Union point to a growing dissatisfaction with the political status quo.

The decline in trust is not limited to political institutions. The media once considered the fourth estate and a pillar of democracy, is now viewed with suspicion by large segments of the population. Accusations of bias, sensationalism, and corporate influence have led many to turn away from traditional news sources in favour of alternative media, which often further exacerbates societal divisions. This fragmentation of the media landscape mirrors the religious and ideological fragmentation seen in late Rome, where differing sects and cults undermined the unity of the empire.

The Dumbing Down of the Populace

In addition to the fragmentation of religion and the erosion of civic duty, one of the most insidious factors contributing to the collapse of public faith is the decline in education. In the later stages of the Roman Empire, the quality of education deteriorated significantly. Classical learning and critical thinking were replaced by rote memorisation of religious texts, and the intellectual elite became increasingly disconnected from the realities of everyday life. This dumbing down of the populace, coupled with the increasing influence of superstition and religious dogma, contributed to the empire's inability to address its pressing challenges.

In the modern West, we are witnessing a similar decline in the quality of education. While the causes may differ, the results are strikingly similar. In many Western countries, educational standards have been eroded by an overemphasis on ideological indoctrination at the expense of critical thinking, history, and the sciences. Instead of fostering a well-informed and engaged citizenry, modern educational systems often produce individuals who are ill-prepared to grapple with the complexities of contemporary society. This "dumbing down" of the populace, whether through a lack of focus on the fundamentals or an overemphasis on ideological conformity, weakens the very fabric of democracy.

The decline in educational standards is particularly concerning when viewed in the context of an increasingly complex and interconnected world. Just as the Roman Empire struggled to maintain its vast territories with an undereducated populace, so too will the modern West find it difficult to navigate the challenges of globalisation, technological disruption, and geopolitical instability with a citizenry ill-equipped to engage critically with these issues.

The Role of Growing Individualism

One of the most significant cultural shifts in both late Rome and the modern West is the rise of individualism. In the Roman Empire, this shift was partly driven by the rise of Christianity, which emphasised personal salvation over collective duty. As religious beliefs became more individualistic, the sense of civic responsibility eroded, leading to a breakdown in social cohesion. The Roman elite became increasingly detached from the needs of the broader population, focusing on their wealth and power rather than the welfare of the state.

In the modern West, individualism has similarly taken precedence over collective responsibility. The rise of neoliberal economic policies in the late 20th century, coupled with the decline of traditional religious and communal structures, has led to a society that prioritises personal success and self-interest over the common good. This growing individualism is evident in everything from the decline of trade unions and community organisations to the increasing emphasis on personal branding and social media. While individualism can be a source of innovation and personal freedom, it can also lead to social fragmentation and the erosion of collective responsibility, much like in the later stages of the Roman Empire.

Lessons from Rome and Potential Remedies (continued)

The collapse of public faith in the Roman Empire was a complex process driven by religious fragmentation, the erosion of civic duty, corruption, and the rise of individualism. These same forces are at work in the modern West, threatening to undermine the very foundations of our societies. However, the lessons of Rome also offer potential remedies, if only we are willing to heed them and make the necessary reforms to restore trust, foster unity, and re-establish a shared sense of purpose.

1. Rebuilding Trust in Institutions

One of the most pressing challenges facing the modern West is the collapse of public trust in institutions be it governments, the media, or even the educational system. Just as the Roman Empire faltered when its institutions became synonymous with corruption and inefficiency, so too will Western democracies struggle if they cannot restore faith in the structures that uphold civic life.

The first step towards rebuilding this trust must involve a genuine commitment to transparency and accountability. Western governments have increasingly become disconnected from their citizenry, fostering a sense of disenfranchisement and alienation. This is particularly evident in how corporate lobbying, special interest groups, and opaque financial dealings have come to dominate the political landscape. Just as late Roman emperors and officials indulged in excesses while neglecting the common welfare, modern Western politicians often appear more concerned with their career preservation or with serving corporate interests than addressing the needs of their populations.

To reverse this decline, political reforms aimed at curbing corruption, reducing the influence of money in politics, and ensuring greater governmental accountability must be a priority. These efforts must be supported by a reinvigoration of democratic engagement at all levels of society, from local to national. Civic participation in political life is key, as it allows individuals to regain a sense of ownership over their communities and nation, and this begins with fostering a more engaged and educated populace (a topic I will return to shortly).

The role of the media in shaping public perception and holding institutions accountable cannot be overstated, both in the context of the Roman Empire and in the modern West. In ancient Rome, the dissemination of information was heavily controlled, and public sentiment was easily manipulated by elites who sought to maintain power and control. This manipulation, combined with limited means of communication, often meant that Roman citizens were kept in the dark about the true state of the empire. A lack of transparency contributed to widespread disillusionment, mistrust, and eventually to the erosion of civic cohesion, as misinformation spread unchecked, and the populace was unable to hold its leaders accountable.

In modern Western societies, the situation is in many ways more complex but no less dangerous. The rise of mass media, coupled with the advent of digital platforms and social media, has vastly increased the amount of information available to the public. However, this has also led to a fragmentation of the media landscape, where misinformation and sensationalism can spread rapidly, often without being subject to the same rigorous standards of truth and accountability that traditional media outlets were once held to. The result has been a significant erosion of public trust in the media, with many citizens feeling that they can no longer rely on mainstream sources for accurate or balanced information.

This is compounded by the ideological bias that has taken root in many Western media outlets. As I have noted, the majority of journalists today tend to lean left politically, and this has had a profound impact on the way news is reported and perceived by the public. Groupthink within the media establishment has led to the perpetuation of certain narratives and viewpoints at the expense of others, often shutting down meaningful debate or dissenting perspectives. This has only served to deepen societal divisions and fuel a growing sense of alienation, particularly among those who feel that their views are being marginalised or misrepresented.

If we compare this to the situation in late Roman society, there are clear parallels. In Rome, the ruling elite controlled much of the information that was disseminated to the public, and they often used this control to maintain their power and influence. This led to a situation where the average Roman citizen was disconnected from the realities of the empire's decline. In modern Western societies, while the mechanisms of control are different, the outcome is similar: a populace that is increasingly distrustful of the institutions that are meant to inform and protect them.

One of the most damaging aspects of this dynamic is how sensationalism has come to dominate much of the media landscape. In the pursuit of clicks, views, and advertising revenue, many media outlets have shifted towards more provocative and sensationalist content, often at the expense of balanced and in-depth reporting. This not only distorts public perception but also exacerbates societal tensions, as divisive issues are highlighted and exaggerated while more nuanced discussions are sidelined.

In Rome, this kind of distortion of public perception contributed to a general sense of instability and disillusionment. As citizens became increasingly aware that they were being misled, their faith in the institutions of the state eroded, paving the way for civic disengagement and the eventual breakdown of social cohesion. Similarly, in the modern West, the erosion of trust in the media has led to a situation where large segments of the population are disengaged from mainstream discourse, instead turning to alternative media sources that often reinforce existing biases and further fragment society.

The rise of social media has exacerbated this problem. Unlike traditional media outlets, which were at least nominally held to journalistic standards, social media platforms operate with little to no oversight. This has allowed misinformation to proliferate at an unprecedented rate, as false or misleading information can be shared widely before it is ever fact-checked or corrected. This is particularly dangerous in an era of deep political polarisation, where misinformation is often weaponised to serve partisan agendas.

Rome, of course, did not have social media, but the parallels are striking, nonetheless. In both cases, the manipulation of public perception by elites or powerful interests led to a decline in civic trust and engagement. In Rome, this took the form of elites using misinformation to maintain their grip on power, while in the modern West, it is often corporate and political interests that use social media platforms to shape public opinion. In both cases, the result is a populace that is increasingly disengaged, disillusioned, and divided.

The solution to this problem, as I would suggest, lies in the media regaining credibility by upholding rigorous journalistic standards, offering balanced perspectives, and avoiding sensationalism. This is easier said than done, however, as the media industry is now deeply entrenched in a system that rewards sensationalism and partisanship. It will require a concerted effort on the part of both media organisations and the public to demand higher standards of journalism and to hold those who fail to meet those standards accountable.

In practical terms, this could mean greater transparency in media ownership, as many large media corporations are influenced by corporate interests that may not align with the public good. It could also mean the promotion of independent journalism, which is often better positioned to offer balanced and nuanced reporting, free from the pressures of corporate advertising or political influence. Furthermore, media literacy should be a priority in educational systems, teaching citizens how to critically assess the information they consume and how to distinguish between reliable and unreliable sources.

In Rome, by the time the population fully understood the extent of the empire's decline, it was too late to reverse course. The manipulation of public perception by elites had succeeded in delaying any meaningful reform until the empire was already on the brink of collapse. In the modern West, we still have the opportunity to correct course, but this will require a fundamental shift in the way we approach media and public discourse. We must move away from the sensationalism and partisanship that currently dominate the media landscape and work towards a system that prioritises truth, transparency, and accountability.

In conclusion, the role of the media in shaping public perception and holding institutions accountable is as crucial today as it was in the Roman Empire. The proliferation of misinformation, combined with ideological groupthink and sensationalism, has led to a collapse of public faith in the media and, by extension, in many of the institutions that underpin Western democracy. To avoid repeating Rome's mistakes, we must restore trust in the media by demanding higher standards of journalism, promoting independent and balanced reporting, and fostering a more critical and engaged citizenry. Failure to do so could see the West follow the same path as Rome, where the manipulation of public sentiment contributed to the ultimate collapse of the empire.

Citizens, too, must be encouraged to consume news critically, discerning fact from opinion or propaganda.

2. Reinvigorating Civic Duty

A key theme that emerges from the decline of both Rome and the modern West is the erosion of civic duty. In Rome, the sense of duty to the state eroded over time, partly due to the growing disconnect between the citizenry and the ruling elite, as well as the weakening of traditional Roman values. Modern Western societies face a similar challenge, where the culture of individualism has in many ways overshadowed the notion of collective responsibility.

To counter this, we must work towards reinvigorating the concept of civic duty. This can be done by promoting community engagement, encouraging public service, and fostering a sense of responsibility towards the common good. Education plays an integral role in this effort. In recent decades, education systems in the West have shifted focus, often emphasising personal achievement and economic utility over critical thinking, civic knowledge, and the development of a sense of shared societal values. As a result, many young people today lack both the historical context and the ethical framework to understand the importance of civic engagement.

Schools and universities must place renewed emphasis on the teaching of history, ethics, and citizenship. By educating the populace on the successes and failures of past civilisations, particularly Rome, we can impart important lessons on the value of collective action and the dangers of neglecting public duty. Similarly, fostering a sense of community from a young age, whether through volunteer programmes, civic education, or youth organisations, can help to reverse the tide of growing individualism and atomisation that pervades modern society.

Moreover, the promotion of voluntary public service whether military or civil could rekindle a sense of duty similar to that once embraced by early Romans. In the past, national service or military duty was seen not only as a means of defending the state but also as a way of fostering loyalty, discipline, and civic pride. A modern equivalent, such as voluntary or compulsory national service in civil sectors, could encourage citizens to reconnect with their communities and help instil a renewed sense of civic responsibility.

3. Addressing Economic Inequality and Corruption

Another key lesson from Rome's fall is the role of economic inequality and corruption in undermining both public faith and social stability. As discussed in previous chapters, the late Roman Empire was characterised by a significant wealth gap between the elites and the broader population, a situation that exacerbated social tensions and eroded the legitimacy of the ruling class. This problem is all too familiar to those living in modern Western societies, where economic inequality continues to rise, and where many citizens feel increasingly disconnected from the political and economic elites who shape policy.

Economic reforms must therefore be central to any effort to rebuild public trust and civic duty. Policies aimed at reducing income inequality, such as progressive taxation, increased social safety nets, and investments in education, healthcare, and infrastructure, can help to create a more equitable society in which all citizens feel invested in the common good. Without addressing the underlying economic disparities that fuel populism, disillusionment, and social unrest, any attempts at restoring public faith will be incomplete.

Furthermore, tackling corruption and financial irresponsibility is paramount. Just as late Roman officials were notorious for their self-enrichment and misuse of public funds, modern political and corporate elites have been implicated in a wide range of financial scandals, from tax evasion to the abuse of public resources. This not only undermines trust in institutions but also weakens the ability of governments to address societal challenges. Comprehensive reforms that increase transparency, limit corporate influence in politics, and hold corrupt officials accountable are essential to reversing this trend.

4. Restoring Faith in Education

A well-educated populace is the cornerstone of any stable and successful society. The Roman Empire's decline was accelerated by the gradual degradation of its educational institutions, as classical learning gave way to rote memorisation of religious texts and a general neglect of intellectual inquiry. Modern Western societies face a similar threat, as education systems increasingly prioritise ideological indoctrination or vocational training over the teaching of history, critical thinking, and the liberal arts.

Restoring faith in education is critical if we are to reverse the decline of public trust and civic duty in the West. Educational institutions must return to the mission of producing well-rounded, critically thinking citizens who can engage with the complex challenges facing their societies. This requires a renewed emphasis on the teaching of history, not as a means of advancing ideologies but as a way of understanding the lessons of the past, particularly the lessons offered by the fall of Rome.

Moreover, education must foster a sense of curiosity, critical inquiry, and engagement with the world. Rather than merely teaching students to regurgitate information, educational systems must equip individuals with the tools to think critically, question assumptions, and engage thoughtfully with differing perspectives. This approach would not only enhance individual agency but also help to rebuild the intellectual foundations of a more engaged and informed citizenry.

5. Rebuilding Social Cohesion Through Shared Values

Finally, if there is one lesson to take from the collapse of Rome, it is the danger of fragmentation whether religious, ideological, or cultural. As Rome's diverse population became increasingly divided along lines of religion, ethnicity, and class, the sense of a shared identity and common purpose dissipated, leading to social instability and, ultimately, the empire's collapse.

The modern West, particularly in the face of globalisation, mass migration, and cultural conflicts, is facing its challenges of cohesion. In previous chapters, I have discussed the role of immigration and cultural integration in contributing to both societal strength and fragility. In this chapter, it is worth emphasising the importance of fostering a shared set of values and a collective identity that transcends these divisions.

While multiculturalism and diversity are often cited as strengths, they must be balanced with the need for societal cohesion. Without a unifying set of values or a common civic identity, societies risk descending into the same kind of fragmentation that contributed to Rome's fall. This does not mean abandoning diversity but rather finding ways to integrate diverse populations into a cohesive societal framework. This could involve promoting a shared civic identity through public education, encouraging intercultural dialogue, and fostering shared values such as respect for democratic principles, the rule of law, and individual rights.

In the Roman Empire, the failure to integrate new peoples and foster a common identity contributed to its collapse. Modern Western societies must avoid this mistake by actively promoting both integration and social cohesion. The success of this effort will depend on the willingness of governments and citizens alike to prioritise unity over division and to seek common ground in the face of cultural, political, and economic differences.

Conclusion: Avoiding Rome's Fate

The collapse of public faith in late Roman society was not the sole cause of the empire's decline, but it played a critical role in hastening its downfall. Today, the modern West faces many of the same challenges: religious and ideological fragmentation, the erosion of civic duty, corruption, growing individualism, and declining public trust in institutions. These forces, if left unchecked, could lead to a similar fate for Western societies.

However, the lessons of Rome also offer a roadmap for renewal. By rebuilding trust in institutions, reinvigorating civic duty, addressing economic inequality and corruption, restoring faith in education, and fostering social cohesion through shared values, the modern West can avoid the same pitfalls that led to Rome's demise. The fate of our societies is not sealed; with the right reforms and a renewed commitment to the common good, we can reverse the tide of decline and secure a stable and prosperous future for generations to come.

Chapter 10: Can Decline Be Reversed? Lessons from Rome and Modern Solutions

History has long taught us that empires rise and fall, each one leaving behind a legacy of triumph and tragedy. The Roman Empire, a colossus that spanned centuries, eventually crumbled under the weight of its own contradictions political, economic, and cultural. But one cannot help but wonder: did Rome's fall have to be inevitable? Were there opportunities to arrest the decline? And more urgently, can the modern West, with its deepening crises, learn from Rome's experience to avert a similar fate?

In this chapter, I will explore the efforts made by late Roman leaders to stave off collapse, particularly the reforms of Diocletian and Constantine, while drawing parallels to the present-day West. We shall examine how their strategies, successes, and failures offer lessons for our own time. Moreover, I will suggest policy recommendations for economic reform, political renewal, and societal cohesion that could help the West navigate its current challenges.

The Reforms of Diocletian and Constantine: Bold but Limited Efforts

By the third century, Rome had already begun showing unmistakable signs of decline much like the symptoms observed in Western societies today. The economy was in disarray, the military was stretched thin, and political instability was rife. In an attempt to halt this downward spiral, Emperor Diocletian implemented sweeping reforms aimed at stabilising the empire. His efforts focused on administrative restructuring, economic intervention, and military reorganisation.

Diocletian's most significant reform was the introduction of the Tetrarchy, dividing the empire into four regions, each governed by a co-emperor. This decentralisation was intended to reduce the burden on any single ruler, thereby creating a more resilient structure. However, while this initially brought some stability, it ultimately contributed to further fragmentation, especially after Diocletian's abdication. The concept of the *Tetrarchy*, instituted by Diocletian in the late Roman Empire, was intended as a solution to the deepening crisis of governance by decentralising power. Faced with the fragmentation of authority, rampant internal divisions, and the constant threat of foreign invasions, Diocletian's creation of a four-ruler system of two senior emperors (*Augusti*) and two junior emperors (*Caesars*) was a pragmatic effort to stabilise the empire by sharing the burden of rule. While initially successful in quelling some immediate issues, the Tetrarchy was ultimately a temporary bandage applied to a far deeper wound: the erosion of centralised authority. The parallels between the late Roman Empire's political fragmentation and the fracturing political systems of the modern West are striking, particularly concerning the European Union (EU) and the federal structure of the United States.

In Rome, the Tetrarchy represented an attempt to address the political chaos that had beset the empire for decades. By dividing the empire into four administrative regions, each ruled by an emperor, Diocletian hoped to bring greater localised control and thus restore order. However, while it may have resolved immediate succession disputes and offered some stability, the Tetrarchy was short-lived. The inherent weakness in this system lay in the fact that it did not address the core problem: the weakening of centralised authority and the rise of competing power structures. Rather than unify the empire, it contributed to further internal conflict as each ruler began to assert dominance over their region, eventually leading to civil wars and a reversion to autocracy under Constantine.

This dynamic is mirrored in the fracturing political systems of today, particularly in the West. In the European Union, we see an experiment in supranational governance that, like the Tetrarchy, was intended to address the challenges of the modern age ranging from economic integration to military and political cohesion. However, the EU, much like Diocletian's system, struggles with its internal contradictions. The governance structure of the EU, particularly the power wielded by unelected bureaucrats in Brussels, reflects a growing centralisation of authority that often bypasses the will of individual member states. This has led to a sense of disenfranchisement among the populations of these nations, fuelling Eurosceptic movements and political instability across the continent.

The criticism that unelected bureaucrats in Brussels make decisions without sufficient accountability to the people of member states is a valid one. It parallels the sense of disempowerment felt by the Roman populace as the empire became more bureaucratic and autocratic in its later stages. The European Union, much like Diocletian's administrative reforms, centralises power in ways that can undermine local sovereignty. Member states often find themselves bound by EU directives and regulations, which are crafted by a relatively small, unelected elite in Brussels, disconnected from the everyday concerns of citizens in places like Poland, Hungary, or Italy. Just as Diocletian's system ultimately failed to reconcile the needs of the empire's diverse regions, the EU struggles to balance the interests of its 27 member states, each with its own unique political, economic, and cultural priorities.

This tension between centralised authority and local sovereignty is a recurring theme in both the late Roman Empire and the modern West. Diocletian's Tetrarchy failed precisely because it could not reconcile the ambitions of multiple rulers within a single empire, leading to competition and, eventually, civil war. Similarly, the European Union faces growing internal dissent from member states that feel their national sovereignty is being eroded by an increasingly powerful and unelected bureaucracy. Brexit is perhaps the most dramatic example of this tension, as the United Kingdom chose to leave the EU in large part because of concerns about the loss of sovereignty and the unaccountable nature of EU governance.

The United States offers another striking parallel. The federal structure of the U.S., with its division of powers between the federal government and individual states, was designed to balance central authority with local autonomy. However, in recent decades, there has been a notable expansion of federal power, often at the expense of states' rights. Much like the Tetrarchy attempted to decentralise power while maintaining centralised control, the U.S. federal government seeks to expand its influence, often through the actions of unelected regulatory agencies. These agencies, such as the Environmental Protection Agency (EPA) or the Federal Communications Commission (FCC), have increasingly imposed regulations that, while not passed by Congress, carry the force of law. This has led to a growing perception that the U.S. federal government is overstepping its constitutional boundaries, much like the bureaucratic overreach seen in late Roman governance.

This phenomenon is particularly evident in the rise of executive orders and regulatory actions that bypass the legislative process. In theory, these agencies are meant to be non-partisan, carrying out the will of Congress, but in practice, they have become powerful actors in their own right, crafting policy and regulations that can have far-reaching consequences. This mirrors the situation in late Rome, where bureaucrats and administrators, often unaccountable to the public, wielded increasing power over the daily lives of citizens. The erosion of the authority of the Senate in Rome, as emperors and their administrative apparatuses consolidated power, is not unlike the growing irrelevance of Congress in the face of expanding executive power and regulatory control in the U.S.

This centralisation of authority and the role of unelected bodies in governance contribute to the broader sense of political disenfranchisement felt by many Western citizens. In both the EU and the U.S., there is a growing disconnect between the governed and those who govern. The rise of populism in recent years can be seen as a direct response to this. There is a clear backlash against what is perceived as an out-of-touch elite that governs without proper accountability to the people.

Rome experienced a similar phenomenon in its later stages. As the empire became more autocratic, with power increasingly concentrated in the hands of the emperor and his inner circle, the Roman Senate and the broader political institutions of the Republic were sidelined. The Roman people became increasingly alienated from their government, and this erosion of civic participation contributed to the eventual collapse of the empire. In the same way, modern Western democracies are seeing a decline in public trust in political institutions, with growing numbers of citizens feeling that their voices are not being heard in the corridors of power. This disillusionment, much like it was in Rome, is a symptom of deeper systemic problems within the political structure.

In the context of the EU, this sense of alienation is compounded by the fact that many of the decisions that shape the lives of Europeans are made by officials in Brussels who are not directly elected by the public. While there are mechanisms for democratic input, such as the European Parliament, the real power lies with the European Commission, which is not subject to direct electoral oversight. This structure can be seen as a modern echo of the late Roman bureaucracy, where emperors and their appointed officials made decisions that affected the empire's far-flung provinces, often without regard for the needs or desires of the local populace.

In the United States, the increasing power of unelected regulatory agencies has sparked similar concerns about the erosion of democratic accountability. The fact that these agencies can issue regulations with the force of law, without those regulations being passed through the legislative process, raises questions about the balance of power within the American political system. This regulatory overreach, much like the bureaucratic inefficiency of late Rome, undermines the principles of representative government and contributes to the growing sense of disillusionment with the political system.

Ultimately, the comparison between the Tetrarchy and modern Western political systems underscores the dangers of centralising power in the hands of unelected bodies while eroding local and individual sovereignty. In both cases, the attempt to impose control from above, whether through Diocletian's administrative reforms or the regulatory frameworks of the EU and U.S., has led to increased political fragmentation, alienation, and ultimately, instability.

The question that arises, then, is whether the West can learn from Rome's failure. One possible solution lies in decentralisation in restoring power to local and regional governments and reducing the influence of unelected bureaucracies. Just as Diocletian's Tetrarchy eventually collapsed because it could not reconcile the tension between centralised authority and local autonomy, so too must the West address the growing discontent with centralised, unaccountable governance. By empowering local governments, respecting the sovereignty of nation-states within the EU, and reining in the power of regulatory agencies in the U.S., the West may be able to avert the fate that befell the Roman Empire.

This restoration of local sovereignty would not only address the political fragmentation seen in the West today but also help to restore public trust in democratic institutions. The lesson from Rome is clear: when central authority becomes too distant and unaccountable, it loses the legitimacy necessary to govern effectively. The West, if it wishes to avoid a similar fate, must heed this warning and find ways to reinvigorate the democratic processes that have been the foundation of its success.

Socialist Price Controls

The issue of price controls as a method of economic intervention, as seen in the Roman Empire under Diocletian and in various modern economies, is a well-trodden path of unintended consequences. Diocletian's *Edict on Maximum Prices* is one of the most famous examples of government interference in the market aimed at curbing inflation. By the third century AD, the Roman Empire was facing severe economic turbulence: rampant inflation, debasement of the currency, and a breakdown of traditional trade networks. Diocletian believed that capping prices for goods and services would stabilise the economy and preserve purchasing power. However, the edict backfired, exacerbating many of the issues it was meant to address. Black markets thrived as traders evaded price controls, shortages became widespread, and public resentment grew. These kinds of policies often deepen the economic problems they seek to solve, as the artificial suppression of prices distorts supply and demand, leading to scarcity rather than relief.

In this regard, there is a stark parallel with modern-day economic interventions in the West, particularly in the United States. The notion of government-imposed price controls has resurfaced in various forms, often framed as a measure to combat corporate greed or price gouging during times of crisis. A notable recent example was the discussion around measures championed by Vice President Kamala Harris to prevent so-called *price gouging*. While the intention behind these interventions may be well-meaning, they reflect the same fundamental misunderstanding of market dynamics that led Diocletian's edict to failure.

In times of crisis, such as during natural disasters or pandemics, demand for essential goods can skyrocket, and with it, prices. This is not, as some political figures might suggest, solely a result of corporate greed but a reflection of the realities of supply and demand. Attempts to cap prices during such periods ignore the fact that higher prices often incentivise suppliers to increase production and distribution, ensuring that goods reach where they are needed most. By imposing price controls, governments risk creating disincentives for production and distribution, leading to shortages much like the consequences experienced in late Roman times.

Moreover, the echoes of Diocletian's policies resonate even more strongly when we consider the broader economic interventions seen in Western countries, such as quantitative easing (QE) and extensive regulatory frameworks. Quantitative easing, initially adopted as an emergency measure in the wake of the 2008 financial crisis, has become a mainstay of Western monetary policy, particularly in the United States and Europe. While it was initially effective in stabilising the financial system, the long-term effects have led to market distortions, asset bubbles, and growing inequality an outcome not dissimilar to the wealth disparities that plagued Rome in its later years.

Just as Diocletian sought to address inflation with price controls but inadvertently stoked further economic instability, modern Western governments have utilised monetary policy and regulatory measures in ways that, in many instances, have exacerbated the underlying problems of economic inequality and stagnation. Quantitative easing, for example, has disproportionately benefited the wealthy by inflating asset prices stocks, real estate, and bonds while doing little to address wage stagnation or the economic struggles of the lower and middle classes. Much as the Roman elites entrenched their wealth and power during times of crisis, so too has QE enriched the financial elites in the West, widening the economic divide.

Similarly, extensive regulatory frameworks, which are often justified as necessary protections against corporate malfeasance or environmental degradation, can have unintended negative effects. Over-regulation can stifle innovation, discourage investment, and make it more difficult for small businesses to compete. This is not to suggest that regulation is inherently bad much like the reforms of Diocletian and Constantine, some level of oversight is necessary to maintain order. However, when regulation becomes overly burdensome, it begins to resemble the bureaucratic inefficiencies of late Rome, where layers of administrative control hindered economic vitality and innovation.

The lessons from Diocletian's failed price controls are further underscored when we compare them to the experience of the Soviet Union. The Soviet system, with its centrally planned economy and fixed prices, serves as one of the most prominent examples of the long-term failures of price control policies. The Soviet Union, much like Diocletian's Rome, aimed to insulate its population from the volatility of markets through strict state control of prices, production, and distribution. However, these policies only exacerbated the inefficiencies inherent in the system. Shortages became endemic, black markets flourished, and economic stagnation set in. By suppressing the natural mechanisms of supply and demand, the Soviet Union eventually collapsed under the weight of its contradictions much as the Roman Empire did centuries earlier.

In the West, there is a growing trend towards the kind of economic controls that echo both Diocletian's edicts and Soviet central planning, particularly in the context of crises such as climate change, healthcare, and housing shortages. While it is crucial to address these pressing issues, there is a real danger that overly aggressive intervention whether in the form of price controls, excessive taxation, or overly restrictive regulation could undermine the very economic foundations that have made Western societies prosperous.

In my earlier chapters, I discussed how economic stagnation and the collapse of infrastructure were key indicators of Rome's decline. These same warning signs are present in the West today, particularly in the context of housing shortages, rising inequality, and the degradation of public infrastructure. Much like Rome's roads, aqueducts, and grain distribution networks, modern Western infrastructure is showing signs of strain bridges, airports, roads, and utilities are in disrepair, while housing shortages in major cities have driven prices to unsustainable levels. Government intervention is often proposed as the solution, but if that intervention takes the form of price controls or overly restrictive regulation, the outcome could be disastrous.

Instead of relying on the blunt instrument of price controls, the West should consider policies that encourage economic dynamism while addressing inequality through more nuanced and market-friendly means. For example, targeted subsidies or tax incentives for essential industries, alongside deregulation where appropriate, could stimulate growth and investment without distorting market mechanisms. Investment in infrastructure, particularly through public-private partnerships, could help to reverse the degradation of public services while promoting innovation and competition.

It is worth noting that one of the central issues facing both late Roman society and the modern West is the problem of inequality. In both cases, elites were (and are) perceived as enriching themselves at the expense of the broader populace. In Rome, this inequality contributed to social unrest, political instability, and ultimately, the empire's collapse. In the modern West, growing inequality has led to the rise of populist movements, widespread discontent, and increasing distrust in democratic institutions. As discussed in Chapter 8, corruption and financial irresponsibility play a central role in this dynamic, as does the misapplication of economic interventions that tend to benefit the few at the expense of the many.

In conclusion, the lessons of Diocletian's price controls, the experience of the Soviet Union, and the current economic interventions in the West all point to the same fundamental truth: markets cannot be controlled without causing further distortions. While governments have a role to play in managing economies, particularly during times of crisis, their interventions must be carefully calibrated to avoid the unintended consequences that inevitably arise when price controls and overly rigid regulations are imposed. The challenge for the modern West, much like it was for Rome, is to strike the right balance between intervention and the free functioning of markets a balance that, if found, could help arrest the decline that so many now fear.

Constantine, Diocletian's successor, is often credited with extending the life of the empire through his embrace of Christianity and the establishment of Constantinople as a second capital. While Constantine's reign did witness a revitalisation of the eastern part of the empire, the west continued its decline. Constantine's reforms, though visionary in some respects, did not address the systemic issues plaguing the empire: political corruption, military overextension, and economic decay. The lesson here is that even bold reforms are not enough if they fail to confront the root causes of decline an insight that Western leaders would do well to heed.

Can the West Arrest Its Decline?

The question before us now is whether the West can arrest its decline. The signs are all too familiar: political paralysis, economic stagnation, cultural fragmentation, and military overreach. Yet history teaches us that decline is not always inevitable at least not immediately. The West has the means and the resources to reverse course, but it will require a concerted effort across multiple fronts: economic reform, political renewal, and societal cohesion.

First, economic reform is essential. The deindustrialisation that has hollowed out the economies of the USA, UK, Canada, and Western Europe must be reversed. Globalisation, while beneficial in certain respects, has led to the outsourcing of manufacturing and the erosion of the middle class. Bringing manufacturing back to home countries would not only create jobs but also restore a sense of economic sovereignty. Additionally, investment in new technologies particularly in engineering, renewable energy, and artificial intelligence could provide the West with a competitive edge in the global economy, much as Rome once benefitted from its superior engineering and infrastructure.

Education reform is another critical area. In recent decades, Western educational systems have drifted away from rigorous standards, prioritising ideology over the foundational subjects of history, mathematics, and critical thinking. This "dumbing down" of the populace has had far-reaching consequences, including a decline in civic literacy and an inability to engage meaningfully with complex political and social issues. In Chapter 9, I explored the role that the loss of public faith in institutions plays in societal decline. Revitalising education and returning to a curriculum that prioritises knowledge, skills, and critical inquiry could help rebuild that trust and foster a more engaged, informed citizenry.

Politically, the West needs a renewal of its democratic institutions. Much like late Rome, where corruption and inefficiency became the norm, the modern West suffers from a political system dominated by special interests, corporate influence, and financial irresponsibility. In Chapter 8, I discussed how corruption accelerates decline by undermining trust in governance. To reverse this trend, political leaders must focus on rebuilding public trust through transparency, accountability, and the elimination of undue influence from lobbyists and corporate donors. This will require electoral reforms, campaign finance restrictions, and perhaps even the introduction of term limits for elected officials a modern counterpart to the administrative reforms attempted by Diocletian.

Finally, societal cohesion must be restored. The moral and cultural decline that I examined in Chapter 4 is a key contributor to the West's fragmentation. Identity politics, the loss of common purpose, and the breakdown of social norms have created a divided and polarised society, much like the late Roman Empire, where different factions and tribes vied for control. To rebuild cohesion, Western nations must foster a renewed sense of civic duty and shared values. This does not mean a return to rigid conformity, but rather a reassertion of the principles that have historically underpinned Western civilisation: democracy, freedom of speech, individual rights, and the rule of law.

Potential Areas of Opportunity

Despite the challenges facing the West, there are opportunities for renewal and growth. Re-industrialisation, as previously mentioned, is one such opportunity. Bringing manufacturing jobs back to Western countries would not only bolster economic growth but also reduce dependence on foreign supply chains, thereby enhancing national security. In a world increasingly shaped by geopolitical competition whether with China, Russia, or other rising powers economic independence will be crucial.

Technological innovation is another area of potential. The West remains a global leader in technological development, particularly in sectors like artificial intelligence, biotechnology, and renewable energy. These industries have the potential to drive economic growth, create jobs, and address some of the most pressing challenges of our time, such as climate change. Much as Rome's advanced engineering allowed it to build roads, aqueducts, and fortifications that sustained the empire for centuries, modern technology could be the key to revitalising the West's infrastructure and ensuring its long-term survival.

Engineering and infrastructure investment will also be critical. As I discussed in Chapter 3, the Roman Empire's collapse was hastened by the degradation of its infrastructure roads fell into disrepair, aqueducts stopped functioning, and trade networks collapsed. Today, Western nations face similar challenges: crumbling bridges, failing water systems, and inadequate public transportation. Investing in infrastructure not only stimulates economic growth but also strengthens societal resilience. Furthermore, this investment could be tied to new, sustainable technologies, creating a modern-day equivalent to Rome's engineering feats.

Global cooperation, while fraught with challenges, presents another potential solution. Much like Rome's dealings with neighbouring tribes, the West must navigate a complex international landscape. However, unlike Rome, which relied on force and coercion, the West has the opportunity to foster cooperation through diplomacy, trade agreements, and multilateral institutions. Climate change, cybersecurity threats, and pandemics are global issues that require coordinated responses. The West, with its historical commitment to internationalism, could lead the way in crafting global solutions that benefit all.

Conclusion: Learning from Rome's Lessons

In conclusion, the decline of the Roman Empire offers both a cautionary tale and a source of insight for the modern West. The reforms of Diocletian and Constantine, though bold, were ultimately insufficient because they failed to address the underlying causes of Rome's decline: political corruption, economic stagnation, military overreach, and cultural fragmentation. These same forces are at work today in the West, but unlike Rome, the West has the benefit of hindsight.

The key to reversing decline lies in recognising these lessons and implementing comprehensive reforms that tackle the root causes. Economic revitalisation through re-industrialisation and technological innovation, political renewal through the restoration of democratic institutions, and societal cohesion through education reform and a renewed sense of civic duty are all necessary steps. While the challenges are daunting, the West is not yet beyond saving. With the right leadership and a commitment to reform, decline can be arrested and perhaps even reversed.

Rome's fall need not be our fate. The empire's warning is clear, but the future of the West is still ours to shape.

Chapter 11: The Future of Western Civilisation: Decline or Transformation?

As I delve into this final chapter, I reflect upon the patterns of history and the pressing concerns of today. As we approach the end of this journey through the rise, decline, and fall of one of the greatest empires in history, it is vital to turn our attention to the question that hangs over our collective heads: Can the West avoid the same fate? As I have explored in previous chapters, the modern West is at a critical juncture, much like Rome was in its final centuries. We see the warning signs all around us economic stagnation, political instability, social fragmentation and must decide whether we will heed the lessons of history or succumb to them.

In this chapter, I aim to offer a vision of what a renewed Western society could look like. A vision not rooted in romanticism, but one grounded in the lessons of history, practical policy, and an understanding of both our strengths and weaknesses. This vision requires a rebalancing of our economies, the reinvigoration of our democratic institutions, and a cultural rejuvenation that can only come from a shared sense of purpose. I will explore the models of renewal we can learn from, both historical and contemporary, and address the global challenges we face, including the growing influence of nations such as China and India, climate activism, and technological disruption. The West's future can be one of resilience and renewal, but only if we are willing to act.

Rebalancing Economies: The Foundation of Renewal

One of the fundamental issues that led to Rome's downfall was the collapse of its economy, a collapse driven by over-reliance on slave labour, inflation, and unsustainable military expenditures. Today, the West faces its own set of economic challenges: growing inequality, stagnating wages, and an over-dependence on the financial and service sectors, particularly in the UK and the USA. The Western economies have become increasingly detached from the industrial and manufacturing base that once made them global powerhouses.

In previous chapters, I discussed how Rome, by the time of its decline, had outsourced much of its agricultural production to its provinces, creating a dependency that eventually crippled its economy. Similarly, the modern West has outsourced much of its manufacturing to countries like China and India, creating vulnerabilities in its supply chains, as evidenced by the COVID-19 pandemic. If we are to reverse our decline, we must bring manufacturing back to our home countries, not out of a sense of nationalism but out of economic necessity. The reinvigoration of local industries would create jobs, reduce dependence on foreign powers, and ensure a more resilient supply chain in the face of global disruptions.

Additionally, we must rethink our economic models to ensure that growth is both sustainable and inclusive. The Nordic countries Sweden, Denmark, and Finland offer examples of economies that balance capitalism with social welfare in a way that promotes both innovation and social equity. These nations have managed to create systems where economic growth benefits a broad spectrum of society, avoiding the extreme inequalities that have plagued the West in recent decades. While these models are not without flaws, they offer valuable lessons in how to create more balanced economies that are resilient in the face of global challenges.

Reinvigorating Democracies: Restoring Trust and Accountability

As Rome's political system became more corrupt, its citizens increasingly lost faith in their leaders, leading to a breakdown in civic duty and social cohesion. In much the same way, the West today faces a crisis of public faith in democratic institutions, as I explored in **Chapter 9: The Collapse of Public Faith**. Citizens are disillusioned by political corruption, ineffectual leadership, and the influence of corporate lobbying, which mirrors the buying and selling of political offices in late Rome. For democracy to survive and thrive, we must restore trust and accountability in our political systems.

One of the first steps towards reinvigorating democracy is reforming campaign finance and lobbying laws to reduce corporate influence on politics. When large corporations and special interest groups hold disproportionate sway over policy, the needs of the average citizen are often ignored. This fuels the populist movements that I examined in **Chapter 5: The Role of Governance**, which arise as a response to perceived governmental failures. While populism can serve as a corrective force, it also carries the risk of pushing democracies towards authoritarianism if not properly managed.

We must also look to examples of successful democratic governance elsewhere. Singapore, though often criticised for its authoritarian tendencies, offers a model of governance that is both efficient and accountable. Its government has a strong track record of long-term planning and execution, which contrasts sharply with the short-termism that characterises much of Western politics. While we should not emulate Singapore's model wholesale, we can learn from its emphasis on meritocracy, long-term planning, and governance by technocrats who prioritise the national interest over personal gain.

Cultural Rejuvenation: Rediscovering Purpose and Identity

The moral and cultural decay of Rome discussed in **Chapter 4: Moral and Cultural Decline**, was a significant factor in its downfall. A society that no longer shares a common purpose or values cannot hold together in the face of external pressures. The West today finds itself in a similar position, with identity politics, cultural fragmentation, and the erosion of traditional social norms leading to a loss of societal cohesion.

A renewed Western society must rediscover a sense of shared purpose and identity, but this does not mean a return to a homogenous culture or the exclusion of immigrant communities. Instead, it requires the cultivation of a civic identity that transcends individual or group identities. This civic identity must be rooted in a commitment to democratic values, the rule of law, and the protection of individual freedoms. At the same time, it must be inclusive enough to embrace the diverse cultures that make up modern Western societies, avoiding the mistakes Rome made when it failed to integrate the large numbers of "barbarian" migrants into its fold.

Education will play a critical role in this cultural rejuvenation. As I discussed in **Chapter 9**, the current trend of teaching ideology over history, mathematics, and critical thinking is contributing to the dumbing down of the populace. A renewed focus on education that emphasises the development of critical thinking skills, a thorough understanding of history, and the ability to engage in reasoned debate is essential for fostering an informed and engaged citizenry. Such an education system would help create the cultural resilience necessary to withstand the social and political challenges of the modern world.

Building Resilient Communities and Infrastructure

As I noted in **Chapter 3: Economic Stagnation and the Collapse of Infrastructure**, Rome's inability to maintain its infrastructure roads, aqueducts, and fortifications was a key factor in its decline. The modern West faces a similar challenge, with ageing infrastructure, underfunded public services, and a lack of investment in new technologies threatening to undermine its long-term prosperity.

Building resilient communities requires not only investing in physical infrastructure but also in social infrastructure. The West must prioritise the development of sustainable cities, robust healthcare systems, and affordable housing to ensure that all citizens have access to the resources they need to thrive. Climate activism, often framed as a threat by some, can catalyze building more resilient communities. Investing in green technologies and renewable energy sources will not only reduce our dependence on fossil fuels but also create new industries and jobs, strengthening our economies in the process.

Moreover, we must address the challenges posed by technological disruption. Automation, artificial intelligence, and other technological advances have the potential to displace large segments of the workforce, creating new inequalities and social unrest. However, with the right policies in place such as retraining programmes, universal basic income, or other forms of social support we can turn these challenges into opportunities. A society that anticipates and adapts to technological change will be far more resilient than one that resists it.

Facing Global Challenges: China, India, and the Future of Globalisation

In **Chapter 6: Military Overstretch**, I explored how Rome's overextended borders and reliance on mercenaries made it vulnerable to external threats. The modern West faces a different set of global challenges but ones that are no less significant. China's rising influence, India's growing economic power, and the ongoing shifts in global power dynamics present both opportunities and threats to the West.

To build a resilient future for the West, we must reimagine our approach to globalisation in a way that addresses the shortcomings of the current model while avoiding the pitfalls of isolationism or protectionism. Much like Rome during its imperial height, the modern West has historically thrived on the back of expansive trade networks and global influence. In Rome's case, the empire's vast trade routes connected Europe, Asia, and Africa, enabling the flow of goods, ideas, and culture. This global interconnectedness was a hallmark of Roman prosperity, as it is today for the West. However, just as Rome eventually struggled to balance the benefits of its vast trade empire with the pressures of managing diverse and far-flung regions, the modern West faced challenges in maintaining the balance between global cooperation and national interest.

The Challenge of Globalisation: Rome and the West

In Rome's later years, the empire increasingly turned inward, focusing on securing its borders and protecting its interests as external pressures mounted. This shift was exacerbated by economic stagnation, as discussed in Chapter 3, where inflation, heavy taxation, and the collapse of trade networks contributed to the decline. Modern parallels can be drawn to the West's recent trends towards protectionism, particularly in the aftermath of the 2008 financial crisis, the rise of populist movements, and the disruptions caused by the COVID-19 pandemic. Isolationist policies, such as trade tariffs, Brexit, and 'America First' rhetoric, echo the kind of defensive posture that ultimately weakened Rome's global reach and economic vitality.

For the West, retreating into isolationism would be a grave error. Like Rome, the West's strength has historically come from its openness to trade, innovation, and ideas from across the world. The Roman Empire, at its height, was a melting pot of cultures and innovations, benefiting immensely from the exchange of goods and knowledge with distant lands. However, as the empire became more insular, it lost this competitive edge. Similarly, in today's globalised world, isolationism risks stifling innovation, reducing access to international markets, and ultimately hastening the decline of Western influence.

A New Approach to Global Cooperation

To avoid this fate, the West must instead seek new forms of global cooperation that prioritise mutual benefit over-exploitation. This requires a fundamental rethinking of how we approach globalisation. Rather than viewing global trade as a zero-sum game, where one nation's gain is another's loss, we must focus on creating trade agreements that are sustainable and equitable. Rome's downfall in part resulted from its inability to maintain the loyalty and cooperation of its provinces, many of which felt exploited and overtaxed by the central authority in Rome. This same sense of inequity can be seen today in the developing world's frustration with the Western-dominated global economic system, which often prioritises the interests of wealthy nations at the expense of poorer ones.

Renegotiating trade agreements to ensure that they work for both developed and developing nations is crucial. The West must take steps to reduce exploitation and ensure that developing countries have access to fair trade opportunities, sustainable development resources, and the means to build their economies without falling into crippling debt or dependence on foreign powers. This not only promotes global stability but also secures the West's long-term interests by preventing the kind of economic and political unrest that can lead to global instability just as the revolts and discontent in Rome's provinces eroded its imperial authority.

Investing in diplomatic relations will also be key. Rome, at its height, maintained a delicate balance of power with neighbouring states, often using diplomacy and strategic marriages to secure its borders and maintain its influence. However, as its diplomatic ties weakened and neighbouring powers like the Germanic tribes grew stronger, Rome found itself increasingly vulnerable to external threats. Today, the West must engage in similar diplomatic efforts, particularly in regions where rising powers such as China are seeking to expand their influence. The West can no longer afford to be complacent or rely solely on its past dominance. Building stronger alliances and partnerships whether through NATO, trade blocs, or diplomatic initiatives will be essential in maintaining global stability and securing the West's place in the international order.

The Competitive Challenge of China

One of the most significant competitive challenges facing the West today is the rise of China, which, much like the rival powers that eventually contributed to Rome's downfall, is positioning itself as a global leader in key areas such as technology, infrastructure, and international diplomacy. In particular, China's ambitious Belt and Road Initiative (BRI) seeks to recreate the kind of vast trade networks that Rome once enjoyed, extending Chinese influence across Asia, Africa, and Europe. At the same time, China is rapidly advancing in critical technologies such as artificial intelligence (AI), quantum computing, and renewable energy, areas where the West risks falling behind.

Rome, in its later years, also faced rising external powers, particularly the Germanic tribes and the Sassanid Empire in the East. These powers were initially seen as minor threats but gradually grew stronger as Rome's internal weaknesses economic decay, political instability, and military overstretch made it more vulnerable to external competition. The lesson here is clear: while external threats may not seem insurmountable at first, they can rapidly become existential challenges if internal decay is allowed to fester.

China's competitive edge is not just about its technological and economic rise but also about its ability to exploit the weaknesses of the West. Just as Rome's enemies used its internal divisions and bureaucratic inefficiency to their advantage, China has become adept at leveraging the open and democratic systems of the West to further its interests. Whether through cyber-espionage, intellectual property theft, or the strategic use of its vast diaspora, China is actively seeking to suborn Western systems and pilfer trade secrets to bolster its position. This kind of strategic competition requires a coordinated and robust response from the West.

To maintain its competitive edge, the West must invest heavily in new technologies, particularly in sectors such as AI, quantum computing, and renewable energy. These are not merely areas of economic competition but fields that will define the future global balance of power. The West's technological superiority, much like Rome's military prowess, has long been one of its defining advantages. However, just as Rome became complacent and failed to keep pace with the innovations of its rivals, the West risks falling behind if it does not prioritise investment in these key areas.

In addition to technological investment, there must be a concerted effort to protect intellectual property and prevent the exploitation of

Western innovations by foreign powers. This will require stronger cybersecurity measures, more robust legal frameworks for prosecuting intellectual property theft, and greater cooperation between Western nations to safeguard their technological and economic assets. Much like the later Roman Empire, which relied increasingly on mercenaries and foreign troops, the West must be cautious about over-reliance on external actors, whether through supply chains or technology-sharing agreements, that could ultimately weaken its strategic position.

Learning from Rome's Mistakes: The Balance of Power

Ultimately, the West's challenge is to avoid the mistakes that led to Rome's fall: overextension, internal divisions, and the failure to adapt to changing global dynamics. Just as Rome overextended its military and economic resources, the modern West must be careful not to spread itself too thin whether through endless military engagements, unsustainable trade deficits, or over-reliance on foreign production.

At the same time, the West must address its internal divisions. Rome's decline was accelerated by civil wars, political infighting, and a general erosion of trust in its leadership. Today, we see similar trends in the form of political polarisation, social unrest, and growing distrust in democratic institutions. These divisions not only weaken the West internally but also make it more vulnerable to external threats, much as Rome's internal discord made it an easy target for its enemies.

In conclusion, to build a resilient future, the West must find a balance between global engagement and self-preservation. Just as Rome's strength lay in its ability to integrate diverse peoples and manage vast trade networks, so too must the West embrace global cooperation while safeguarding its interests. By investing in new technologies, protecting intellectual property, and renegotiating trade agreements in a way that promotes mutual benefit, the West can maintain its competitive edge in the face of rising powers like China. However, this will also require addressing the internal divisions and structural weaknesses that threaten to undermine Western civilisation from within. Just as Rome fell due to a combination of external pressures and internal decay, so too will the West if it fails to learn from the lessons of history.

A Future Worth Fighting For

The Roman Empire's fall was not inevitable, nor was the decline of the West. However, as I have demonstrated throughout this book, history offers stark warnings that we would be foolish to ignore. Rome's downfall was the result of a combination of factors economic stagnation, political corruption, military overstretch, and moral decay and these same forces are at work in the modern West. Yet, unlike Rome, we have the benefit of hindsight, and with that comes the opportunity to change course.

Reimagining prosperity in the West will require difficult choices and bold actions. We must rebuild our economies to be more inclusive and resilient, reinvigorate our democratic institutions to restore public trust, and foster a renewed sense of shared purpose that can bridge the cultural divides threatening to tear us apart. By learning from both the mistakes and successes of history, we can chart a course towards a future that is not only prosperous but also sustainable and just.

The challenges are immense, but the rewards of success in a more resilient, equitable, and united Western society are well worth the effort. The future is still ours to shape, and we must seize the moment to build a civilisation that will stand the test of time.

What lessons can we glean from the fall of the Roman Empire, and how do they inform the trajectory of Western civilisation? Are we, like Rome, on an inevitable path towards collapse, or is there still hope for transformation and renewal? The answer, I believe, lies somewhere in between. History may not repeat itself, but it certainly rhymes, and the parallels between Rome and the modern West are too stark to ignore.

The Roman Empire, at its peak, seemed invincible. Its military might, economic prowess, and cultural dominance stretched across much of the known world. Yet, as I explored in Chapter 1, the empire's zenith was merely the precursor to its decline. The same could be said of the West in the post-World War II era, when the USA, UK, Canada, and Western Europe stood as the unquestioned leaders of the global order. But as with Rome, cracks in the foundation began to emerge.

The fall of Rome was not a single, catastrophic event but rather a gradual process of decay, as outlined in Chapter 2. Political corruption, economic stagnation, and military overextension all played their part, as did the empire's inability to integrate the waves of migrants that poured across its borders. These same issues plague the modern West. Many of the warning signs of Rome's decline are evident in the contemporary landscape: rising inequality, political polarisation, and a loss of public faith in institutions, as I discussed throughout the earlier chapters of this book. The question now is whether these signs signal an irreversible decline or if they can serve as the impetus for transformation.

Predictions Based on Historical Patterns and Current Trends

If history is any guide, decline seems inevitable. Empires rise, reach their zenith, and eventually fall, often due to internal rot as much as external pressures. Rome's decline was exacerbated by its overextended borders, corruption within its leadership, and the gradual erosion of civic duty and faith in public institutions. In Chapter 9, I examined how the collapse of public faith in the Roman Empire mirrors the secularisation and loss of civic responsibility seen in today's West. The proliferation of individualism, the dumbing down of educational standards, and the erosion of public trust in media, government, and even economic structures all point to a similar trajectory.

Moreover, as I noted in Chapter 7, mass migration played a pivotal role in Rome's downfall. The empire's inability to assimilate or integrate the vast numbers of newcomers led to internal fractures. Today, the West faces similar challenges, with migration spurring social cohesion concerns and cultural conflicts, particularly where the values of incoming populations differ from those of the host nations. As history has shown, a society that cannot integrate newcomers risks division, and these divisions can be fatal to an empire's survival.

Yet, while the patterns of history are undeniable, the future is not set in stone. The West today has resources, technology, and knowledge that Rome could never have imagined. The question, then, is whether we can harness these tools to reverse or at least mitigate the decline.

Exploration of Possible Futures

In contemplating the future, several possible scenarios emerge, each shaped by current trends and potential shifts. One path is that of continued decline, much like Rome. If the West continues on its current trajectory of rising inequality, deepening political polarisation, unchecked corporate influence, and ongoing cultural fragmentation the result will be a slow and steady descent into irrelevance. This would be a future marked by the erosion of democratic norms, the weakening of global influence, and the eventual collapse of infrastructure and public services, as I explored in Chapters 3 and 8.

However, another possibility is that the West transforms, triggered by either necessity or choice. A geopolitical shift, such as the rise of China or India as dominant global powers, could spur the West into action, forcing it to adapt or face obsolescence. In such a scenario, we might see a technological revolution, one that reinvigorates economies, creates new industries, and fosters a cultural renaissance. The West has historically been a hub of innovation, and this capacity for reinvention should not be underestimated. From the Industrial Revolution to the digital age, the West has shown a remarkable ability to adapt to changing circumstances.

A third future, and perhaps the most optimistic, is that of a cultural renaissance. Just as the Renaissance of the 14th to 17th centuries saw Europe emerge from the so-called Dark Ages, the West today could experience a revival of civic virtue, intellectual curiosity, and artistic achievement. This renaissance would not merely be a return to past glories but a reimagining of what Western society could be. Such a transformation would require a fundamental shift in values a rejection of materialism and individualism in favour of community, responsibility, and a renewed sense of purpose.

This path, however, is fraught with challenges. In Chapter 4, I explored the moral and cultural decline that plagued Rome, and how similar forces are at work in the West today. The rise of identity politics, the breakdown of social norms, and the loss of a shared cultural identity all undermine the cohesion necessary for such a renaissance. Yet, history has shown that societies can change, even in the face of seemingly insurmountable odds.

Final Thoughts on the Long-Term Outlook for Western Civilisation

So, can the West adapt, or will it follow the Roman Empire into history? The answer depends largely on whether we can learn from the past. Rome fell not because of a single event but because of a series of interconnected failures economic, military, political, and cultural. These same challenges face the West today, and if we are to avoid a similar fate, we must address them with a sense of urgency.

At the heart of the matter is governance. In Chapter 5, I discussed how Rome's weak and ineffective leadership contributed to its downfall, and the same can be said of many Western nations today. Political leaders seem more concerned with short-term gains and partisan politics than with the long-term health of their societies. If we are to reverse the decline, we need leaders who are willing to make difficult decisions, to put the needs of the many above the interests of the few, and to work towards building a more just and resilient society.

Economically, the West must also confront its growing inequality and the disintegration of its industrial base. In Chapter 10, I explored the potential for reversing economic decline through policy reforms, such as returning manufacturing to home countries and investing in new technologies and education. These steps are essential if we are to build a resilient future, one that can withstand the pressures of globalisation, technological disruption, and shifting geopolitical landscapes.

Culturally, the West must find a way to rebuild a sense of shared identity and purpose. The fragmentation that has accompanied the rise of identity politics, as discussed in Chapter 4, has weakened social cohesion and undermined the sense of common purpose that once united Western societies. A cultural renaissance, as I mentioned earlier, is not beyond our reach, but it will require a renewed commitment to civic duty, education, and the arts.

In the end, the future of Western civilisation is not predestined. Decline is a possibility, but so too is transformation. The question is whether we have the will to make the necessary changes, learn from the mistakes of the past, and build a future that is resilient, just, and vibrant.

This chapter serves as the final meditation on the central theme of this book: what Rome's fall tells us about the West today. As I have explored throughout these chapters, the parallels between the two are striking, but they are not inevitable. We have the benefit of hindsight, the tools of technology, and the capacity for change. The future is ours to shape if only we dare to do so.

Epilogue

As I conclude *The Empire's Warning: What Rome's Fall Tells Us About the West Today*, I am reminded once more of the immense weight of history and the responsibility it imposes upon those who live in its shadow. Growing up in England, walking Hadrian's Wall and exploring Roman *Vindolanda*, I felt the distant echoes of a civilisation that had once been so powerful, so certain of its place in the world. The ruins stood as monuments not only to Roman greatness but also to the impermanence of even the mightiest of empires. That sense of impermanence has never left me, nor should it leave any of us as we consider the current state of the West.

We, too, live in a time of extraordinary power and accomplishment, much like Rome in its zenith. Yet, as we have seen, the signs of decline are also all around us. Edward Gibbon's great work on the fall of Rome was more than a history it was a warning. He chronicled how corruption, moral decay, political instability, and economic stagnation slowly eroded the foundations of an empire that once seemed invincible. In this book, I have drawn these parallels to the modern West, not to prophesy doom but to provoke reflection and inspire action.

One of the key lessons I have sought to impart through these pages is that decline is rarely sudden. It comes in stages, often unnoticed or ignored until it is too late to reverse. For Rome, the tipping point may have come with the rise of internal division, the breakdown of civic duty, or the relentless waves of migration that challenged the empire's capacity to integrate. For us, the warning signs are no less clear. Whether in the form of crumbling infrastructure, declining public trust in democratic institutions, or the rise of populist movements reacting against ineffective governance, the threads holding Western civilisation together are fraying.

But while the story of Rome's fall is a tragedy, our future need not be. As I have discussed in the final chapter, we still have the potential to transform rather than decline. Unlike the Romans, who lacked the foresight of history, we can draw upon their experiences and the experiences of countless other civilisations that rose and fell when charting our course. It is within our power to learn, adapt, and reimagine the future.

In the chapter *Can Decline Be Reversed?* I explored how we might address the economic, political, and social fractures that threaten the stability of the West. The lessons of Diocletian and Constantine, while ultimately unsuccessful in saving the Roman Empire, still offer valuable insights into the necessity of bold reform. For us, such reform could take many forms reshoring manufacturing to restore economic independence, embracing technological innovation to drive growth, and reinvigorating our educational systems to cultivate a new generation of thinkers, builders, and leaders.

Yet reform alone is not enough. The collapse of public faith, detailed in *The Collapse of Public Faith: Religion, Civic Duty, and Decline*, remains one of the greatest challenges of our time. Without a shared sense of purpose, without the civic spirit that once bound Rome together in its early days, no amount of economic or political reform will save us. We must, as a society, rediscover the values that have historically sustained civilisations through times of uncertainty and crisis duty, responsibility, and a sense of belonging to something greater than ourselves.

In contemplating the future of Western civilisation, I have often returned to the ruins of Roman Britain. What lessons do they offer for us today? They remind us that even the greatest empires can falter, that power and wealth are fleeting, and that the very things we take for granted can disappear in an instant if we are not vigilant. But they also remind us of the incredible resilience of human beings. Even after the fall of Rome, Europe eventually found its way back to the light through the Renaissance, through technological and scientific advancements, and through the rediscovery of classical knowledge.

This is the vision I offer for the West. Not one of decline, but of renewal. In the chapter *The Future of Western Civilisation: Decline or Transformation?* I speculated on what a renewed West might look like rebalanced economies, vibrant democracies, and cultural rejuvenation. We can rebuild, draw upon our rich intellectual and cultural heritage, and forge a new path that avoids the mistakes of Rome.

But renewal requires both leadership and collective will. It requires us to confront the uncomfortable truths about our current trajectory and to make the difficult choices that will set us on a better course. It requires the courage to look at our societies not with complacency, but with urgency. We must ask ourselves: Are we content to drift into irrelevance, as Rome once did, or are we willing to take the steps necessary to ensure that our civilisation endures?

As I leave you with these final thoughts, I am neither a pessimist nor a blind optimist. The story of Rome is a cautionary tale, but it need not be our destiny. Whether the West follows Rome into history or emerges from its present challenges transformed will depend on the choices we make today. In the end, the fate of our civilisation rests not in the hands of fate, but in our own. The future is still unwritten.

End

Did you love *The Empire's Warning: What Rome's Fall Tells Us About the West Today*? Then you should read *The Dragon's Gambit: China's Bid for Global Dominance and the Western Response*[1] by John Shenton!

[2]

In the 21st century, few challenges loom as large on the global stage as the rapid rise of China, and it's bid to assert dominance in every sphere of international influence. The Dragon's Gambit: China's Bid for Global Dominance and the Western Response provides a detailed, multifaceted exploration of this phenomenon, offering readers a critical examination of China's strategic ambitions and the global repercussions. This book does more than recount history—it dissects China's current manoeuvres, scrutinizing the far-reaching consequences and posing urgent questions for the West's response.

---

1. https://books2read.com/u/bzyZ9E

2. https://books2read.com/u/bzyZ9E

Also by John Shenton

Business Plan Basics

The Bahamas - More Islands and Recipes Than You Expect!

Collected Musings from Bricks and Mortar to E-commerce

The Smart City Odyssey: Unveiling the Secrets to Traveller-Centric Software

The Dragon's Gambit: China's Bid for Global Dominance and the Western Response

Silent Weapon

Business Basics: Money Sources

Influx

Fried Chips

Mandates, Motors, and Misinformation

Echos of Orwell

Control and Chaos

The Empire's Warning: What Rome's Fall Tells Us About the West Today

About the Author

John Shenton was born in Birmingham, England and grew up in postwar England. He spent several years as a Radio Officer onboard a variety of vessels sailing to the Persian Gulf, the Indian Ocean and South China seas.

With degrees and a background in electronics and computers he has lived and worked within the United Kingdom, Germany, Switzerland and Canada.

While doing so, he established numerous trading relationships in Japan, Korea, the USA, China and other countries.

He has been retired for some time now living in Montréal Canada enjoying golfing, writing, sailing and many other things automotive.

About the Publisher

John Shenton published via Draft2digital